Penguin Books

The Philosophical Quest

Brenda Almond is Reader in Philosophy and Education at the University of Hull. She was born in Liverpool and studied philosophy under A. J. Ayer. She has subsequently held appointments at various universities in the United Kingdom, as well as visiting appointments in West Africa, Australia and the United States. She has lectured widely – in Canada, Sweden, Poland, Germany and Spain. She is Chair of the Society for Applied Philosophy and joint editor of the *Journal of Applied Philosophy*. Her books include *Moral Concerns, Education and the Individual, Means and Ends in Education* and *AIDS: A Moral Issue*.

D0104345

The Philosophical Quest

Brenda Almond

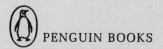 PENGUIN BOOKS

PENGUIN BOOKS

Published by the Penguin Group
Penguin Books Ltd, 27 Wrights Lane, London W8 5TZ, England
Viking Penguin, a division of Penguin Books USA Inc.
375 Hudson Street, New York, New York 10014, USA
Penguin Books Australia Ltd, Ringwood, Victoria, Australia
Penguin Books Canada Ltd, 2801 John Street, Markham, Ontario, Canada L3R 1B4
Penguin Books (NZ) Ltd, 182–190 Wairau Road, Auckland 10, New Zealand

Penguin Books Ltd, Registered Offices: Harmondsworth, Middlesex, England

First published as *Self-Starters: Philosophy* 1988
10 9 8 7 6 5 4 3 2

Typeset, printed and bound in Great Britain by
BPCC Hazell Books
Aylesbury, Bucks, England
Member of BPCC Ltd.
Typeset in Linotron 202 Melior

To T.M.

Contents

Three passions, simple but overwhelmingly strong, have governed my life: the longing for love, the search for knowledge, and unbearable pity for the suffering of mankind.

. . . Love and knowledge, so far as they were possible, led upward toward the heavens. But always pity brought me back to earth. Echoes of cries of pain reverberate in my heart. Children in famine, victims tortured by oppressors, helpless old people a hated burden to their sons, and the whole world of loneliness, poverty and pain make a mockery of what human life should be.

Bertrand Russell,
The Autobiography of Bertrand Russell: Volume I,
1872–1914
(London: Allen & Unwin, 1967)

Preface

Philosophy is too large a subject to be trapped and pinned down within the covers of a book like this. All that is possible is to give an impression of what it involves. I have chosen to do this by describing a kind of pilgrim's progress, or journey of exploration through some of the paths and by-ways of philosophy. In this way I hope the whole subject will be seen, even if briefly and inadequately, through one person's eyes. But who, you may ask, is this person?

You will find the pronoun 'I' scattered quite freely throughout these pages. So you may, if you wish, take it that the person who is this 'I' is the author. But if so, then you should not assume this to be simply another instance of the authorial 'I' used to hand down received lore to would-be initiates. Better, though, if you regard the 'I' in these pages as a third person – neither you nor I – a seeker engaged in a quest, asking questions which do not have accepted answers. This seeker will move on step by step, sometimes reaching conclusions, sometimes remaining in doubt. If you, the reader, would care to stand beside the seeker in this exploration, then you need not be constrained by either the conclusions or the doubts that emerge. Feel free to disagree. For the first principle of philosophy is simply this: form your own judgement.

A note here on practicalities: you may, if you wish, read the text as continuous, chapter by chapter, and follow the sequence of reflections set out there. In this way you will have made contact, by the end of the book, with many contemporary debates in philosophy.

Several large topics, though, are touched on in passing. To indicate these, there is a system of notes and references, together with a Reading Guide, at the end of each chapter. Refer to the notes for information about the general theme of each chapter and about reading in specific topics. The Reading Guide is a key to the academic literature on the subjects covered. The books listed there are first steps only in each field and, in most cases, they themselves contain further bibliographies and detailed references which you may pursue according to interest, taste and time.

Acknowledgements

In writing this book, I have benefited greatly from the hospitality of the Philosophy Department in the Faculty of Arts at the Australian National University during a period of leave from the University of Surrey. I should like to thank colleagues there and in the Research School of the Social Sciences for their advice, criticism and encouragement.

I owe an inestimable debt to three people in particular for reading and commenting on the whole manuscript stage by stage. These are: J. J. C. Smart, Peter Forrest and Thomas Mautner. I have also appreciated comment on individual chapters from Genevieve Lloyd and Richard Campbell. For fulfilling the invaluable role of supplying a 'starter's' perspective with enthusiasm and interest, I should like to thank Martin and Paula Cohen.

My thanks are extended to Christopher Strachan who translated the passage from Epictetus in Chapter 7 especially for this book. I am grateful, too, to Chris Falzon for assistance with research and with the compilation of bibliographies, and to Kanthi Fernando, Reta Gear and Jean Ryan, secretaries in the Philosophy Department at the Australian National University, for typing the major part of the book.

1 A Starting Point

> You will not learn from me philosophy, but how to
> philosophize, not thoughts to repeat, but how to think.

– Immanuel Kant

There cannot be a thought without a thinker. So since philosophy, for most people, represents thought at its most abstract, it is worth reflecting that people – not excluding philosophers – begin by thinking about themselves and their personal concerns before they move on, if they do at all, to profound reflection or broad speculation in the sciences, arts or philosophy. So let us – I, the writer, you the reader – try to conform to this natural order, and follow the path from the personal to the philosophical, from the specific to the abstract.

This means that we need as a starting point a person who cares. A person concerned about herself (or himself) and about the world; a person seeking answers to questions that don't have straightforward practical answers. Without this, philosophy can have no intrinsic appeal, although it might have some market-value in a world where most academic accomplishments have a use and a price. We might begin by asking: what sorts of questions seem worth asking in this way? Answering this question could be a path towards an understanding of philosophy.

But as a preliminary ground-clearing operation it would be useful to begin by setting aside one popular idea of what philosophy is. This use of the term can probably best be recognized by the presence of the definite or indefinite article. Or by the fact that it can also be used in the plural. So people talk of a philosophy or alternative philosophies, meaning by this systems of answers, whole frameworks of thinking which settle once and for all a person's response to situations or problems that come along. In this sense there can be not only philosophies of life but also particular professional philosophies – a philosophy of medicine, for example, or a philosophy of education. By contrast, the sense in which philosophy is the subject of this book is the sense in which the word is used without prefix – neither *a* philosophy, nor *the* philosophy – and the sense in which it does not have a plural. This is philosophy pure and simple; understood like this, it describes not a system of beliefs but a method, an attitude or an approach. It deals in questions rather than in answers, problems rather than solutions. All the same, it would be a mistake to assume that the process of asking questions philosophically, even if it *begins* in doubt, must inevitably end that way.

Taking philosophy as a method rather than as a system of beliefs, there can still be a difference in approach which centres on this question of open-endedness or commitment. Recent philosophy in the English-speaking world, for example, has tended to follow in an empiricist tradition: the tradition, that is, that bases substantial knowledge on what can – or at least might in principle – be observed by sight, touch, hearing and the other senses. One distinction in particular that has been emphasized is that between facts – the kind of things that *can* be observed by the senses – and values, which cannot be. As a result, a style of doing philosophy has emerged which aims to leave moral pronouncements to others, preserving its own neutrality; at the same time, as far as other areas of inquiry are concerned, scepticism, which is the admission of defeat in the quest for knowledge, has become something of an occupational hazard, and its refutation is the theme of many philosophers working within this tradition.

But philosophy as a method need not be centred on this distinction, and indeed the original model of philosophy as a method was provided many centuries ago (in Athens in the fifth century BC) by the people whose activities and discussions prompted the coining of the term 'philosophy' in its original meaning of love of wisdom. In this original setting, the activity amounted, in the most general terms, to a willingness to pursue an argument to its conclusion, challenging it at every stage and seeing it as always open to refutation. This stance in itself involves a double commitment: first, commitment to the truth (the point of rejecting conclusions which can be shown to be false is to arrive at some which may be reckoned to be true); and secondly, commitment to certain moral virtues implicit in such a method: honesty, openness and impartiality – terms which inescapably lead to some notion of moral right, justice or moral good. But, of course, a double commitment of this nature may well mean that sometimes conclusions are drawn as well as questions asked.

The questions, though, are quite distinctive. Once you have said that they lack straightforward practical answers, you have eliminated many questions that might otherwise have been considered candidates. And yet as human thought has developed over the centuries into its present highly specialized areas, many questions of this eliminable sort *have* been classified as philosophical. The first philosophers in the Western philosophical tradition did not make distinctions of this kind. They were omnivorous consumers of all that could satisfy their cosmic curiosity. They were concerned with questions about the nature of reality, about the 'stuff' or fabric of the universe, about the difference between seeming and reality; they were intrigued by paradox and fascinated by mathematics. Some of these are still matters for philosophy; but, as practical ways of answering questions have emerged, many of these areas of questioning have been split off as sciences or bodies of knowledge in their own right, leaving philosophy with only the residue of unanswered questions. (The term 'natural philosophy' is still used in the titles of some ancient university chairs as a name for physics, and such studies as psychology and sociology have only recently – that is, within the last century – emerged as areas where systematic methods of solving problems make them sciences rather than areas of speculation.)

So this preliminary negative definition considerably narrows the field. Scientific, factual and historical questions lie outside the present-day scope of philosophy. But that still leaves other questions that strike many people as questions of first importance. The double commitment mentioned suggests a way of categorizing these residual questions. They are questions about value, and questions about truth. For while a scientific question like 'What is the melting-point of gold?' does have, even if it has to be qualified, a straightforward way of arriving at an answer, the question 'How do I know that the resulting – or any other – scientific claim is true?' is very much more problematic, and is rightly seen as belonging to the province of philosophy, rather than to that of the science in question. More exactly, indeed, it would be right to describe it as a question in the philosophy of science. And while quantum physicists may reach agreed conclusions as to how to create nuclear fission, questions about the use of nuclear power or nuclear weapons are questions about value and areas for moral judgement. In either case, there may be conceptual questions – for example, the question What *is* scientific knowledge? – or even purely verbal questions – for example, Does 'gold' always mean the same thing? – which will need to be settled first. But even a right understanding of the language will only tell us how our ancestors, who framed our language, construed the world, so the contribution from the analysis of language must be limited both on the question of truth and, even more, on the question of value.

Nevertheless, the starting point for any list of questions which, lacking agreed methods of solution, are potentially questions for philosophy might well include some which relate to meaning and language. But many other questions beginning 'How do I know that . . .?' will feature as well. Apart from the problem of justifying scientific knowledge, and apart from questions that seek a moral direction for action, there are inquiries which at first sight *look* as if they *might* be settled by observation, but on reflection it seems that they can't. For example: how do I know that a friend and associate is a person of sensibility and feeling? I know how *I* feel when I hear an old tape of Jelly Roll Morton. No doubt it would be a mistake to infer that my friend feels the same. But when he sees a fine sunset? Or has to go to the dentist? Is slighted or treated with contempt? Is mugged, tortured or abused? Other people's responses to questions about their feelings may be matters for psychology, or social anthropology. But justifying claims to know about the feelings themselves – and whether they exist at all other than as names given to noises emerging from a black box – remains essentially an issue for philosophy.

But seeing other people as people is not merely an exercise in philosophical reasoning. It is also a matter of intuitive feeling, empathy and awareness. Take, for example, the following passage from

Paul Scott's *The Jewel in the Crown*, which illustrates strikingly how, without this empathetic awareness, or this human intuition, whole classes of people – in this particular case a whole race – may simply not have attributed to them the feelings which are extended to others. After Kumar, an Indian educated at a British public school, has been systematically ignored by the assistant and also by the other (white) customers, Scott writes:

> It was at this period, after the visit to the pharmacy, that the notion of having become invisible to white people first entered his head, although it took some time for the notion to be formulated quite in this way. When he had become used to crossing the river from the bazaar to the railway warehouse and used to the way English people seemed to look right through him if their eyes chanced to meet his own, the concept of invisibility fell readily enough into its place, but still more time was needed for that concept to produce its natural corollary in his mind: that his father had succeeded in making him nothing, nothing in the black town, nothing in the cantonment, nothing even in England because in England he was now no more than a memory, a familiar but possibly unreal signature at the end of meaningless letters . . .[1]

So the fact that people can fail to attribute to other people feelings similar to their own, and that this is not the sort of mistake that pulls you up short like failing to notice a glass door which is in your way – a self-correcting mistake – is not merely an occasion for logical puzzlement. On the contrary, it has significant consequences for practice – consequences with an essentially moral aspect. Other examples bear out this point. Where torture is institutionalized, torturers are expected, in the interests of efficiency, to refer to and to think of their victims as numbers rather than names, and may be instructed to avoid looking at the face, particularly the eyes. Similarly, it is significant that firing-squads and executioners are usually presented with a blindfolded or hooded victim. It is quite possible, then, not to recognize the person in another human body.

So if there is knowledge about other people as centres of consciousness, this is not going to be the kind of knowledge that emerges as a result of reasoning through a tight deductive argument; neither is it likely to be the product of a further gathering of facts about what people say or do. Just as a scientific description of an experiment on a laboratory animal may simply record paroxysms, muscular spasms, and similar indications of extreme pain without any actual reference to pain, in exactly the same way other human beings *could be* and sometimes *are* regarded in this dispassionate way. It seems that if a name is to be given to the kind of knowledge that may be involved in the case of either humans or animals, it might have to be described as intuitive knowledge.

This is not to put a large question mark over the claim, or to single out other people's, or animals', feelings as particularly dubious. For I may be able to make out no better case than this for recognizing my *own* feelings and selfhood – and yet this is hardly something I could question. I must accept my notion of myself as a starting point for thought. This is, though, not a *bare* notion of myself at this moment in time but a notion of myself as a continuing being. And this suggests another range of reflections which I cannot immediately see how to answer. How am I to account for my notion of myself *as a continuing being* – my self-awareness? How can I justify it? At first, the factor I single out is my memory, which links the child I remember being with the person I now am.

But then I reflect that there would still be a continuous person, even if I lost my memory or became senile or confused. So I conclude, perhaps, that my self is simply a continuing body – a physical object in the world – whose history can be tracked back in space and time to the infant that emerged from its mother's body on a particular day in a particular place. But it is difficult to regard myself *only* in this light. This, after all, is first and foremost what my 'self' is to others. *I* seem to have a different kind of experience of 'self'. So is this experience or knowledge to be called 'intuitive', too?

But already, in discussing this last problem, a number of other questions have begun to crowd in – questions which must also be classified as philosophical if the test for this is not having straightforward practical answers; what, for example, *is* a 'physical object'? In classifying my body, or that of another person or animal, as a physical object, I may be implicitly making all kinds of claims I couldn't substantiate either by observation (looking, listening, touching, etc.), or by simple argument (pure reasoning without factual input).

What sort of claims might these be? Calling something a physical object seems to involve the claim first of all that there is something constant there – something that does not simply reappear each time I give my attention to it. Secondly, I suppose that I call this thing an object in the outside world, not just a figment of my imagination, because I want to assert that it is something that strikes other people in much the same way as it does me. Then, thirdly, it seems to be implied of this something that it is the kind of thing that, while it may reveal itself at one moment to just *one* of my senses – I may simply be looking at it just now, for example – it *could* be felt, smelled or listened to as well, as appropriate. In other words, what looks like a simple assertion about a fairly ordinary thing – tree, house, table – is actually an extremely complex and controversial claim involving reference to a great variety of present and future situations.

What is more, when I look further into my own beliefs, I see that I am, perhaps unconsciously, setting the object against a background of space. I single it out from some vague backcloth on which I can register position and shape. But do I have a notion of space? As children sometimes amuse themselves with indefinitely expanding addresses, ending up with their town, their country, the world and the universe, perhaps I experiment with setting an object, mentally, against an extending background of this sort: a leaf design with vase as background; vase with wall as background; wall as part of house; house against country landscape; country landscape encompassed finally by the boundaries of my vision, but located in a particular part of the earth–globe, itself set in a universe, set into . . .? Even if I can fill *that* gap by reference to astrophysics, it seems that eventually I must end up with a gap I really cannot fill, but, what is more, with no very clear idea of what kind of difficulty this is.

Then, in talking about my self I referred to memory, and thus to time. So, first of all, and in general terms, how can I justify reliance on my memory? How is it that memory gives – if it does – access to the past? Can I afford to deny that it does this, or would that denial involve the breakdown of every other claim I make to knowledge? Both a continuing self and a continuing object are notions that involve a reference to time, and both involve at least a small span of memory recall. But what is the notion of time in which we locate talk about the self or about objects?

It may be that these are all in the end to be described as special kinds of knowledge. Or perhaps they are to be seen as presuppositions for thinking about anything at all. But certainly if there are any distinctively philosophical questions, they are these. It is not just the questions themselves, though, but also the way they are approached, that marks out philosophy from, say, poetry, mystical reflection, science or mathematics. Philosophy begins, it seems, when these questions, which a child or an unreflective person might think had easy answers, begin to be seen as puzzles. St Augustine (AD 354–430), for example, prefaced his philosophical reflections on time with the words 'What then is time? I know well enough what it is, provided that nobody asks me; but if I am asked what it is and try to explain, I am baffled.'[2] In other words, seeing that there is a question may be a more accurate indication of distinctively philosophical concern than having an answer.

As this last illustration suggests, though, what philosophers do is itself probably the best clue to what philosophy is. So it might be useful to begin by looking at one or two examples of the way in which philosophers have approached questions concerning truth, knowledge and justification. This may reveal something of the commitment involved in deciding to approach questions philosophically, or from the philosophical point of view. In the first of these examples, the philosopher Socrates (b. 469 BC), who was put on trial in Athens in 399 BC and was subsequently put to death, makes a reasoned defence of his life as a philosopher. The extract is from the speech he made at his trial (called the *Apology*). Socrates has been described as philosophy's first martyr, and this extract may be regarded as the earliest known statement of the way in which the occupation of philosophy is to be pursued. Plato (428–348 BC), who was present at the trial, made a written account of this speech, as he did of other conversations of the historical Socrates, and, having once established the dialogue form as a way of writing about philosophy, went on to employ it more creatively, using it later as a vehicle for his own rather than Socrates' ideas.

Socrates suggests that his judges might say to him, 'Tell us about your occupation; tell us what it is that you do'; and he proceeds to give them this account of the background to his philosophical activities and of the form that it took:

> I have gained this reputation, gentlemen, from nothing more or less than a kind of wisdom. What kind of wisdom do I mean? Human wisdom, I suppose. It seems that I really am wise in this limited sense . . . Now, gentlemen, please do not interrupt me if I seem to make an extravagant claim, for what I am going to tell you is not my own opinion. I am going to refer you to an unimpeachable authority. I shall call as witness to my wisdom, such as it is, the god at Delphi.
>
> You know Chaerephon, of course . . . Well, one day he actually went to Delphi and asked this question of the god – as I said before, gentlemen, please do not interrupt – he asked whether there was anyone wiser than myself. The priestess replied that there was no one . . .
>
> When I heard about the oracle's answer, I said to myself, What does the god mean? Why does he not use plain language? I am only too conscious that I have no claim to wisdom, great or small. So what can he mean by asserting that I am the wisest man in the world? He cannot be telling a lie; that would not be right for him.
>
> After puzzling about it for some time, I set myself at last with considerable reluctance to check the truth of it in the following way. I went to interview a man with a high reputation for wisdom, because I felt that here if anywhere I should succeed in disproving the oracle and pointing out to my divine authority, You said that I was the wisest of men, but here is a man who is wiser than I am.
>
> Well, I gave a thorough examination to this person – I need not mention his name, but it was one of our politicians that I was studying when I had this experience – and in conversation with him I formed the impression that although in many people's opinion, and especially in his own, he appeared to be wise, in fact he was not. Then when I began to try to show him that he only thought he

was wise and was not really so, my efforts were resented both by him and by many of the other people present. However, I reflected as I walked away, Well, I am certainly wiser than this man. It is only too likely that neither of us has any knowledge to boast of, but he thinks that he knows something which he does not know, whereas I am quite conscious of my ignorance. At any rate it seems that I am wiser than he is to this small extent, that I do not think that I know what I do not know . . .

After this I went on to interview a man with an even greater reputation for wisdom, and I formed the same impression again, and here too I incurred the resentment of the man himself and a number of others . . .

The effect of these investigations of mine, gentlemen, has been to arouse against me a great deal of hostility, and hostility of a particularly bitter and persistent kind. But the truth of the matter, gentlemen, is pretty certainly this, that real wisdom is the property of God, and this oracle is his way of telling us that human wisdom has little or no value. It seems to me that he is not referring literally to Socrates, but has merely taken my name as an example, as if he would say to us, The wisest of you men is he who has realized, like Socrates, that in respect of wisdom he is really worthless.

But Socrates' view of wisdom was not as negative as this might sound, and towards the end of his speech he went on to say:

If you put me to death, you will not easily find anyone to take my place. It is literally true, even if it sounds rather comical, that God has specially appointed me to this city, as though it were a large thoroughbred horse which because of its great size is inclined to be lazy and needs the stimulation of some stinging fly. It seems to me that God has attached me to this city to perform the office of such a fly, and all day long I never cease to settle here, there, and everywhere, rousing, persuading, reproving every one of you. You will not easily find another like me, gentlemen, and if you take my advice you will spare my

> life. I suspect, however, that before long you will awake
> from your drowsing, and in your annoyance you will take
> Anytus' advice and finish me off with a single slap, and
> then go on sleeping till the end of your days, unless God
> in his care for you sends someone to take my place.[3]

As things turned out, of course, the Athenians *did* take Anytus'
advice and *did* finish off Socrates with a single slap, and indeed
attempted not many years later to do the same for Aristotle. This
could be taken as an early warning that philosophy – in the sense of
stripping oneself and others of the comfortable old clothes constituted by the tired presuppositions with which one normally con-
fronts life – can be a dangerous occupation. The double commitment
already mentioned reveals itself very clearly in Socrates' speech: to
truth, on the one hand; to virtue – doing what is right, and avoiding
evil – on the other. The second commitment comes over even more
strongly in another part of the speech, when Socrates says:

> You are mistaken . . . if you think that a man who is worth
> anything ought to spend his time weighing up the pros-
> pects of life and death. He has only one thing to consider
> in performing any action – that is, whether he is acting
> rightly or wrongly, like a good man or a bad one.

If Socrates' speech, then, strikingly illustrates the second commitment of philosophers, the following passage from the French philosopher René Descartes (1596–1650) is a fine example of the first. It
demonstrates Descartes' commitment to the stripping away of presuppositions in even the most secure areas of thinking:

> Some years ago I was struck by the large number of false-
> hoods that I had accepted as true in my childhood, and
> by the highly doubtful nature of the whole edifice that I
> had subsequently based on them. I realized that it was
> necessary, once in the course of my life, to demolish
> everything completely and start again right from the foun-
> dations if I wanted to establish anything at all in the
> sciences that was stable and likely to last . . .
>   But to accomplish this, it will not be necessary for me
> to show that all my opinions are false, which is something

I could perhaps never manage. Reason now leads me to think that I should hold back my assent from opinions which are not completely certain and indubitable just as carefully as I do from those which are patently false. So, for the purpose of rejecting all my opinions, it will be enough if I find in each of them at least some reason for doubt. And to do this I will not need to run through them all individually, which would be an endless task. Once the foundations of a building are undermined, anything built on them collapses of its own accord; so I will go straight for the basic principles on which my former beliefs rested.

Whatever I have up till now accepted as most true I have acquired either from the senses or through the senses. But from time to time I have found that the senses deceive, and it is prudent never to trust completely those who have deceived us even once . . .

What is more, since I sometimes believe that others go astray in cases where they think they have the most perfect knowledge, may I not similarly go wrong every time I add two and three or count the sides of a square, or in some even simpler matter, if that is imaginable? . . .

I have no answer to these arguments, but am finally compelled to admit that there is not one of my former beliefs about which a doubt may not properly be raised; and this is not a flippant or ill-considered conclusion, but is based on powerful and well-thought-out reasons. So in future I must withhold my assent from these former beliefs just as carefully as I would from obvious falsehoods, if I want to discover any certainty . . .

I will suppose therefore that . . . some malicious demon of the utmost power and cunning has employed all his energies in order to deceive me. I shall think that the sky, the air, the earth, colours, shapes, sounds and all external things are merely the delusions of dreams which he has devised to ensnare my judgement. I shall consider myself as not having hands or eyes, or flesh, or blood or senses, but as falsely believing that I have all these things. I shall stubbornly and firmly persist in this meditation; and, even if it is not in my power to know any truth, I shall at least do what is in my power, that is, resolutely guard against assenting to any falsehoods, so that the deceiver, however powerful and cunning he may be, will be unable to impose on me in the slightest degree.[4]

What these two extracts reveal, then, is a technique which is the distinctive hallmark of philosophy: a willingness to strip the mind bare of preconceptions, of received opinion, and to follow a path forward that is not laid down by any external authority, which imposes its own constraints, and which is not to be deviated from because the going is uncomfortable, or the results look unattractive or make the person pursuing them unpopular.

It is not surprising that this commitment to truth, when harnessed to the kind of honesty or moral firmness that will not consider compromise, runs people up against the barriers – which may be legal and political – of other people's prejudices. There is, for example, the power of consensus, the tyranny of fashion and the prestige which attaches to 'hard' scientific knowledge, as compared with moral or philosophical reflection. These may operate as constraints on thinking quite as powerful as those – largely religious – which applied in the past. Then, many writers of philosophical works were obliged to pay lip-service to a belief in God which did not quite square with the rest of their beliefs. Descartes himself, for example, had carefully to make it clear that his sceptical thinking was merely an experiment conducted to see how he would reason if he did *not* have the benefit of faith. Religion today may still present a harsh face of dogma and enforcement hostile to the truly open pursuit of inquiry, especially if it is institutionalized in a religious state – this despite the fact that honesty and commitment to truth are compatible with an enlarged understanding of religion in at least some of its forms.

At the same time, major political systems which are entirely secular in their foundations may provide a setting which is as hostile to a pursuit that involves being able to think freely as that of any religious state. One result of this is that philosophy, more than any other academic discipline, may even in contemporary societies provide a focus for dissent within a closed political system and may, indeed, provide a rallying point for people from diverse political settings. In Prague recently, for example, the Czech police repeatedly attempted to suppress unofficial gatherings of intellectuals committed to the study of philosophy. Seminars and lectures in private houses were broken into, arrests made, and philosophers obliged to flee the country or remain to pursue their interests in an atmosphere of secret surveillance and risk to job, security and physical safety.[5] The situation, however, had a parallel in Poland where a 'flying university' was known even in the days of the tsars.[6] More recently in South America, gatherings of people committed to the study of philosophy met under another kind of repressive regime in an attempt to found an unofficial philosophy institute. These examples transcend local and temporal settings and frameworks and display philosophy as a highly general enterprise of the human mind, which everywhere and at all times struggles to free itself of the shackles imposed by closed systems of thought.

The person, then, who provides the starting point here – the concerned person, who may be you, the reader, reflecting on your own life, the state of the world and the kind of questions which lack obvious answers – is already bound by the double commitment – the commitment to virtue and the commitment to truth – to avoid any uncritical acceptance of an all-embracing ideology. A critical acceptance may be a later possibility. For the moment, however, this must be the point of departure. It will be interesting to see how far it can take us.

Notes to Chapter 1

1. Paul Scott, The Jewel in the Crown (St Albans: Granada, 1973, p. 254). A similar theme occurs in Ralph Ellison's novel The Invisible Man (1952): 'I am an invisible man . . . I am a man of substance, of flesh and bone, fibre and liquids – and I might even be said to possess a mind. I am invisible, understand, simply because people refuse to see me.' The general question of how we may be justified in reasoning by analogy from our own case to the conclusion that others, too, have thoughts, feelings and sensations like our own has been a major interest of recent

analytic philosophy. For a discussion of the nature of mind and of mental attributes, see Chapter 6.

2. St Augustine, *Confessions*, Book XI, sec. xiv. The difficulty in explaining time starts from the fact that all our measurements of time depend on cyclical events, such as movements of the hands of a clock, the rotation of the sun, the alternation of day and night, the sequence of seasons. For temporal reference we select an arbitrary fixed point – the birth of a leader, for example, or some other unique or memorable event. Consequently, it may seem that time is a matter of the relationship of events, only to be defined relatively, and that the notion of absolute time is meaningless. But if we accept this, we risk losing touch with some important anchor-points in our understanding of our own experience: the idea of the movement or flow of time, for example, and the assumption that time has a direction, closing off the past and leaving the future open. To these problems may be added the difficulties involved in assuming either that time is made up of measurable moments, no matter how short in duration, or on the other hand that any 'moment' of time is infinitely divisible.

3. Plato, *Apology*, selected passages.

4. Descartes, *First Meditation*, selected passages.

5. See, in relation to this, Alan Montefiore's review of H. G. Skilling's *Charter 77 and Human Rights in Czechoslovakia*, in *Journal of Applied Philosophy* 1, 1984.

6. For an account of this, see N. Davies, *God's Playground* Vol. II, pp. 234–5.

Reading Guide to Chapter 1

There are many introductions to philosophy. The best one to read first would be Bertrand Russell's *Problems of Philosophy*. There are also:

Anthony O'Hear, *What Philosophy Is*

G. Vesey (ed.), *Philosophy in the Open* (written in dialogue form)

B. Magee, *Men of Ideas*

M. Hollis, *An Invitation to Philosophy*

A number of the specific topics touched on in this chapter – our knowledge of other minds, the self, problems of perception, for example – are discussed by A. J. Ayer in his books *The Problem of Knowledge*, *Foundations of Empirical Knowledge* and *Central Questions of Philosophy*. See also J. J. C. Smart, *Problems of Space and Time* and B. Williams, *Problems of the Self*. Most of these questions feature, too, in L. Wittgenstein's *Philosophical Investigations*, which would, on its own, provide a stimulating way into philosophy for the adventurous.

For the history of philosophy, see Bertrand Russell, *History of Western Philosophy* or, for a shorter and selective account, R. Scruton, *A Short History of Modern Philosophy*. For reference there is F. C. Copleston's long and comprehensive *A History of Philosophy* in a new 3-volume edition, or D. J. O'Connor, *A Critical History of Western Philosophy*. For more recent developments, see J. Passmore, *A Hundred Years of Philosophy*, with its sequel, *Recent Philosophers*.

But the best place to begin would not be with any of these, but by reading the dialogues of Plato relating to the trial and death of Socrates, in particular the *Apology*, *Crito* and *Phaedo*, and then reading Descartes' *First Meditation*.

2 Looking Inwards

> *All the interests of my reason, speculative as well as practical, combine in the following three questions:*
>   *1. What can I know?*
>   *2. What ought I to do?*
>   *3. What may I hope?*
>
> —Immanuel Kant,
> *Critique of Pure Reason*

The first and most pressing question for a reflective person determined not to operate unthinkingly on the sole basis of received opinions is likely to be the question: what shall I do? This means that the second and third questions posed by the German philosopher Kant (1724–1804) will almost certainly take precedence over the first. Indeed, they may be supplemented by another, which is equally personal. This fourth question is difficult to formulate, but it is the question which might be answered by following the instruction carved over the entrance to the oracle at Delphi (the one consulted by Socrates' friend) – 'Know yourself.' Whatever that brief and enigmatic instruction was meant to convey, it would surely evoke a response in most people. For most people do have a primary interest in their own person and concerns. And if they want to understand what lies outside themselves – Kant's first question – still more, gain some kind of mastery or control over it, then it is reasonable to suppose that they may have to begin by understanding themselves and gaining some kind of control over their own lives.

The attempt at control necessarily begins, though, with personal decision-making which is the outcome of reflection on the question: what shall I do? This is a question that everyone must ask, explicitly or implicitly, because action is unavoidable, where speculation about what exists is not. Of course, the question is not a request for a prediction, but rather a weighing of competing possibilities for action. And so it may equally well be expanded to: what is the right thing to do? But that is a question open to an even wider variety of interpretations. For example, suppose that someone has made a promise, on the strength of which someone else has made various irreversible and life-affecting decisions. The feelings of the person who made the promise change. 'What is the right thing to do?' here may mean 'What is the *convenient* thing to do?' – that is, from the point of view of the person who made the promise. Alternatively, however, it might be a way of considering the convenience of the person to whom the promise was made. Again, asking what is the right thing to do might be a way of considering whether there is a *mutual* point of view which would be the best for both parties. Finally, asking what is the right thing to do might mean none of these, but something which ignores the question of convenience altogether. Used in this way, it coincides with Kant's second question; 'What ought I to do?' And it is when someone wonders whether there *is* a viewpoint outside convenience – what might be called a moral point of view – that distinctively philosophical reflection about personal life begins.

Self-interest

But moralizing is a rather unpopular pursuit; for this reason, if no other, it might seem at first sight worth trying to avoid judging situations or making decisions on the basis of morality. Better, perhaps, or at least more rational, to take expediency in some form or other as the deciding factor. In particular, I might ask, what is wrong with self-interest as a guide to action? Indeed, do I really have the capacity to act on any other basis? I know from my own experience what it is to present a sham front to the world; to do the kind or the charitable act for wholly selfish reasons. Perhaps it is a form of self-deception to think I ever do anything from any other motive. If this could be true of myself, then what, I wonder, lies behind the mask of charity or kindness that other people present? Perhaps again this naked self-interest. Everyone is what he is as a result of a unique combination of heredity, upbringing and social influences. Is there any room for anything else? Anything one could call a moral motive?

It was an implicit assumption of both moral philosophy and religion in the past that if people were to be expected to act rightly, then they would need to be persuaded that it would at least not cut across their best interest. So Plato and Aristotle (384–322 BC) hoped to show that morality, or virtue, would be for a person's long-term good. If you could get away with murder, Plato asked in the *Republic*, why shouldn't you?[1] (He answered his own question by arguing that on a deeper, more considered view of the situation you couldn't 'get away' with murder – evil-doing is a disease that destroys your own personality and so your happiness.) Subsequently, Christian theologians were anxious to offer at least a happy after-life as some compensation for the sacrifices moral rectitude might demand in this one.

To some extent this seems a reasonable idea. Personal happiness does not require a great deal of argument to commend it. Already, however, both the Platonic and the Christian viewpoint seemed to assume a notion of happiness which differs from the obvious. Happiness, on both of those accounts, was consistent with being poor, ill, badly treated by other people, perhaps even killed. So the sense in which I agree that happiness is an obvious goal is clearly not the sense in which those positions support me. Of course, if pursuing my own personal interest coincides with doing right in a moral sense, there is no problem.[2] But if I take these two views as guides, I can only suppose that doing right may make extraordinary demands on me in the ordinary run of life, even if some final and ultimate compensation is being held out either in this life or the next.

So I will suppose for the moment that the sense in which I might consider taking self-interest as my guide and yardstick is the obvious sense in which day-to-day individual decisions may be made on that basis, rather than some reinterpreted long-term sense which may not even apply until after my death. And here I notice some problems with the arguments of those who favour it. To begin with, if someone argues that I *ought* to consult only my own interest in deciding what to do on any particular occasion, then this suggests a belief that I have the option of doing otherwise. So the person who thinks that external causes account for everything I do, and that I am pre-programmed to follow rational (or even irrational!) self-interest, can't be the same person who thinks self-interest the appropriate guide to action. This second position presupposes a choice. Once I notice this, I can look at the two questions separately:

1. Is there only self-interest?

This question itself has a double aspect:

(i) Must *I* act only from self-interest? Do I really have choices, including that of not being selfish? It seems a sufficient answer to this to say that I am strongly aware that I *have* sometimes been motivated by awareness of another person's need, or distress, etc. I *have*, metaphorically as well as actually, given presents (although some people give only nicely calculated 'exchange gifts'). So much for myself.

But I can also ask:

(ii) Must I assume exclusive self-interest in others?
In trying to answer this, I reflect that I can see a very clear difference between, for example, Albert Schweitzer (who devoted much of his life to medical work in Africa) and the Marquis de Sade (whose recommendations and reflections may have inspired some peculiarly brutal child-murders in Britain in the 1960s) – and between either of these and a playboy whose ostentatiously self-indulgent life-style I read about in the Sunday supplements. I can also appreciate the altruism of, say, a pilot who remains with his plane, even though he might have saved his own life by ejecting earlier, in order to steer his plane away from a school playground or populated area. If he was aware that the result of that decision would be his own death, then – belief in an after-life apart – that action must be regarded as altruistic. So if philosophers, economists and people who work in advertising agencies try to persuade me that selfishness is universal, then I feel justified in dismissing the arguments which lead them to their conclusion (if they have arguments, and are not merely making unsupported assertions) in the face of examples like these.

This means that I will not feel compelled to accept that the end-result of reflecting on my own life and of asking questions about the right thing to do must be an answer in terms of self-interest. I can see that it might be possible to reinterpret self-interest so drastically that it could demand a good deal of what would usually be described as self-sacrifice of me, but that is another matter. I can also see that there could be a way of interpreting 'self-interest' so that *whatever* I decide in the end is in a trivial (tautological) sense, my own choice – my own decision – and therefore my 'interest'. But it seems doubtful whether much would be gained by distinguishing between real and apparent altruism, real and apparent selfishness, in this way. The 'apparent' sort seems to have all the hallmarks of the real, and its practical consequences are indistinguishable. So, in the obvious sense that interests me, the question of whether I, or others, *must* follow self-interest can be answered in the negative. I do have a choice.

There remains the second question:

2. *Should* I take self-interest as my guide?

Once I have established that there are alternatives, this suggestion loses much of its appeal. There are, after all, other people whose happiness matters to me, to put it no higher. I am also impressed by the arguments of those who point out how elusive a quality personal happiness is – that the more you pursue it directly, the less likely you are to find it. And so, if I *can* select goals in life, why confine myself to this narrow one, particularly since it is bedevilled by this built-in paradox?

But there are problems not only in relation to myself and my own course of action. If I choose self-interest as my guide, what am I to recommend other people to do? A world in which *everyone* pursues his or her own personal interest and well-being does not sound an attractive one for *me* to live in; but I can hardly try to maintain consistency by recommending other people to pursue *my* good.

It seems, then, that the question, 'what is the right thing to do?', does not have to be answered in terms of narrow self-interest. Maybe expediency *is* involved – but, if so, it must be a wider expediency than this.[3]

The common interest

Supposing, then, that I say: the right thing to do is to aim at the best possible outcome in any situation. I mean by this that I should look at the consequences of alternative courses of action and then make my decisions on the basis of trying to produce the happiest, most satisfactory outcome, not just for myself, but for all who may be affected by them. Although at first sight an attractive suggestion, working out the application of this principle is not as straightforward as I may initially expect. An individual action or decision is like a stone that I cast into a pond with an indefinitely extending ripple-effect. How limited a view should I take of consequences? Should I restrict my attention to those that happen in the next few hours? Or the next few days? Or should I have a much longer-term perspective than that? And *whose* involvement should I count? My own, of course. But beyond that? Do I stop with the immediate circle of those directly involved, or should I look beyond those relatively narrow limits to the wider community?

I can see that the answer I get to the question, 'What is the right thing to do?', might well be different in these different cases. It is not difficult to think of an example. Perhaps I offer to drive someone home. *That* must be right in terms of mutual satisfaction. But perhaps there is an accident and the other person is injured. Now, in the same terms – the happiness of those directly involved – it was, on the contrary, the *wrong* thing to do. But then suppose that, as a result of his lifelong disablement, the other person promotes a cause – a disablement charity, for example, which provides inestimable improvements in the lives of many others. Do I now say that my original action was right after all? This case illustrates the difficulty of deciding where and with whom consequences stop. But it also reveals another important point: that there is a different between judging an action on the basis of its *actual* consequences and judging it on its *intended* consequences. If I – very reasonably – decide that only the second can be my concern, then I have in fact moved from the idea of morality as promoting some outcome, and switched to the idea of morality as an inner attitude – a matter of motive rather than achievement. And if this is so, I cannot but ask whether this – aiming for the happiest outcome – is in fact the best and only motive available to me. Shouldn't I also consider questions of justice and entitlement – particularly those entitlements I may myself have created by making promises? And shouldn't I also give special weight to the interests or expectations of people specially close to me –

people I am in a distinctive and unique way responsible for, such as spouse, companion, child, parent, friend? May I manipulate other people or withhold from them what is their due?

Then, I know that in practice the word 'necessity' has been used to justify atrocity rather than to limit it, despite people's best intentions. (For example, the Hague Convention – the very convention that was intended to limit use of the more horrendous weapons of war – by introducing the term 'unnecessary suffering' opened the way to an interpretation which fell in practice on the question of military *necessity* rather than military restraint.) This makes me suspicious of any general argument for ends justifying means. So finally I ask whether what I hope to achieve will justify *anything*, no matter at what cost for others? If I believe, for example, that by planting a bomb in a café, supermarket or school playground I can bring about a revolutionary change that will be for everyone's long-term good, is my belief and my motivation a sufficient justification for the suffering I cause to the few individuals randomly affected by my act? Does *their* view of it matter? Where does my responsibility begin and end?

One of the problems with a view which focuses on consequences in this way is that actions can be valued only for their *causal* properties. This means that many otherwise appalling deeds become thinkable if they feature as links in a favoured causal chain. I see *myself*, too, only as an instrument, and the notion of 'knowing myself', and being responsible only for the manageable here and now that I can see clearly, becomes lost in a wider, more indefinite perspective. The view that promotes the goal of the common interest, when formulated as a full-blown theory, I can recognize as the one known to moral philosophy, political theory and economics as utilitarianism. As a movement for legal, political and social reform in the early nineteenth century it had much to recommend it, but as a guide to a personal ethic it has serious limitations. Jeremy Bentham (1748–1832) and John Stuart Mill (1806–73), both of whom offered classic expositions and defences of the theory, were clear that it was not, in a sense, a theory that could be argued *for*. 'That which is to prove everything else', said Bentham, referring to the principle of utility, 'cannot itself be proved.'[4] And Mill wrote: 'Questions of ultimate ends are not amenable to direct proof. Whatever can be proved to be good, must be so by being shown to be a means to something admitted to be good without proof.'[5] The question is, then, whether, as an answer to 'What shall I do?', promoting happiness or doing what is best for everyone concerned, is the best possible guide to action and personal life-style. Two features of the view that it is are that (a) it makes right depend on results, and (b) it takes it that pleasure or happiness is the only value. Both these assumptions seem sufficiently questionable for me to consider whether there might not be an alternative viewpoint, one reached, perhaps, by reversing both these assumptions.[6]

The interest of morality

I return to the case of the person who has made a promise on which someone else has relied. If promoting the happiest outcome for all concerned were the only thing involved there, it would be a puzzling question as to why a promise should have been made in the first place. The two people could have agreed on a policy of promoting the happiest outcome without talking about promises or committing themselves in advance to a course of action which might in the end *not* be for the best for everyone when the time came. It seems, in this case, that the nature of the action is as important as – perhaps more important than – its likely consequences. The very fact that a promise is involved, that the actions involved can be described as the keeping or the breaking of a promise, seem relevant considerations to set against effects and results, and the keeping of trust seems an item of value as well as the happiness of the parties. In literature and life duty has frequently been set against inclination; and while it would be convenient if it could be shown that following the first would in the long run promote the second, it may be necessary to consider the revolutionary suggestion – first made by Kant – that, whether this be so or not, morality, understood as the viewpoint of duty, provides its own point and purpose – that there is, in other words, such a thing as a moral interest.

How, though, should I interpret the 'moral interest'? It is some answer to this to say that when it comes to other people's dealings with me, I know what it is to object to some course of action by saying 'But you promised' or 'It would not be fair' or 'That's unjust'.

The problem with deciding on the right thing to do always in terms of the consequences was that that policy seemed to leave these other kinds of consideration out of account altogether. What is more, it seems that no description of the facts (either the ones that exist at present or the ones I may bring about by my actions) could possibly *determine* what my response should be. It appears, then, that what the 'moral interest' encompasses, and what I am seeking, may be some *principles* for action. Where should I look for them?

Both religion and cultural tradition are possible sources, but if I were likely to be content with either of these, I would not be raising these questions. Both represent the acceptance of authority. My search is for something that has an intrinsic appeal to *me* – something that compels my rational acceptance. And since some such initial commitment is needed for a person to accept a religious or traditional viewpoint in the first place, this requirement is in any case probably not one I could do without altogether, even if I did in the end favour one of these authority-based solutions.

But can there be an independent standpoint? The one that Kant himself suggested was one defined simply by rationality – a reason-based morality reached by setting aside all purely personal or ephemeral wants and desires and all immediate inclination. The test of the rightness of a course of action would then become its universality or scope. 'I ought never to act', Kant wrote, 'except in such a way that I can also will that my maxim should become a universal law.'[7]

Kant held that this principle could be applied so as to demonstrate the wrongness of, for example, lying or breaking promises, by a simple process of reasoning. A thought-experiment in which these become universal laws of action actually breaks down, he suggested, because by applying the 'universal law' test it becomes clear that both lying and promise-breaking are parasitic on telling the truth and on keeping one's word – without this as the norm they are empty or meaningless concepts. Can I imagine a universal practice of telling lies or breaking promises whenever convenient? Kant's insight was not that this would be undesirable, but that it cannot even be carried through in imagination.

So, looked at from this point of view, a programme for action based on principles may be more rationally defensible than one based on maximizing happiness, or doing the best for everyone concerned in the context of a particular situation. Does this mean, then, that there is a moral standpoint from which statements like 'this would be wrong' become true or false? Does it mean that moral principles are in some sense waiting to be discovered and that moral obligations are to be viewed as externally binding on human beings? Is the answer to 'What is the right thing to do?' to be found by consulting a brief but teachable set of principles like the Ten Commandments or the Sunna – principles to which everyone has access through something that might be described as conscience, or an inner light?

In some respects principles are, of course, admirable. A man or woman of principle is, on the whole, to be respected. But the reverse side of the coin of this firmness and steely predictability must be an inflexibility, a lack of human responsiveness and sympathy which is not so unreservedly admirable. But this is not the only problem with principles. There is also, first, the fact that principles do not always point in the same direction; for example, I may be torn between the duty to keep a promise and the obligation to spare someone's feelings. Why should one, rather than the other, principle be given priority? And then, secondly, it is very clear that not everyone is in fact agreed on any particular set of principles. I have to recognize that there is a whole range of issues of principle which divide person from person: abortion, surrogacy, mercy-killing, capital punishment and so on. So, where the first of these objections was concerned, conscience seems to be unclear in its deliverances; and, as far as the second is concerned, it seems hard to appeal to conscience at all, since it is difficult to see why its deliverances should vary so drastically from person to person.

All these considerations point away from locating the moral interest in a narrow set of fixed principles for action.[8] Nor does it seem necessary to do this. For while the promotion of good may be controversial, and duty may generate dilemmas, these do not exhaust the ways in which the moral interest may be represented. Recognizing that some things are bad, for example, may be less problematic than recognizing others as good; agreement on rights may be less elusive than agreement on principles. And if the idea of a cold and empty abstract morality of rules or principles lacks appeal, and the notion of 'ought' is fraught with difficulties, it may be possible to get more purchase on the notion of evil and on the idea of value as the other side of that particular coin.

This is at least in part because it is easier to be sure of recognizing pain and suffering in another human being than of identifying happiness. And the link between, on the one hand, causing pain and suffering and, on the other, displaying evil or wickedness, is far more clear-cut than that between causing happiness and being good.[9] This means that I can begin to see an answer to my own question as to what I should do, which, as it happens, meets the 'Kantian' requirement that I can readily extend it as a demand that I make of other people too. This is an answer initially defined in negative rather than positive terms. Since I can see that the most undisputed evils and the grossest forms of wickedness – for example, genocide, judicial murder, torture and exploitation – are a result of some people's abuse of others, I am ready to accept that I should recognize boundaries within which other people may operate, unhindered by my interference or molestation. I should recognize others, that is, as people, and define their boundaries in moral terms. What name can I give to this notion? The most obvious way to describe it would be as the recognition of rights. Perhaps, as far as I am concerned, recognizing others' rights will still give me a morality of duties, but these will take their origin in the other person, rather than in my own pursuit of virtue. But on their own, rights and reciprocal duties will not be enough to provide a complete answer to my question. The language of rights is limited and negative; and so the positive and the wider answer I am seeking may need the addition of another notion, that of value.

Rights and values

Traditionally, moral philosophy dealt in perfect and imperfect duties. A language of rights and values reproduces this to some extent. A complete or 'perfect' obligation may be involved when what is in question is repaying a debt; a commitment of a more voluntary or 'imperfect' nature is involved when it comes to doing a stranger a good turn or contributing to a charitable cause, something which has *value* as an act of kindness. The first someone has a *right* to demand of me; the second may evoke gratitude and appreciation.

The first I can demand of everyone else similarly placed; the second I may admire in others, but cannot demand of them.

The language of rights, then, seems to express very well the limitations on choice applying to my actions in relation to other people. Certain choices would be an invasion of the right of others to enjoy the degree of self-choosing autonomy that I need for myself, in order both to ask and to answer my initial question,'What should I do?' In particular, of course, a morality based on rights will rule out the most flagrant abuses of other people's personality. But it may be a relevant consideration, too, on a more personal, domestic or intimate scale. The general question that I ask is: can I set limits to the ways in which I may act towards other human beings? And it seems to me that I may do this by reflecting in the case of any particular issue on the area in which I myself claim freedom to act.

But if I decide to act on a basis of respecting the rights of others, at the same time attaching value to certain personal characteristics and perhaps, too, to certain states of affairs (very often those where happiness is a main component), am I not laying myself open to a variety of charges? Perhaps it will be said that rights and values are baseless notions, that they come from nowhere, have no justification. Perhaps it will be said that they have validity, but only in the context of my own social setting – or even for me alone and not for anyone else. Perhaps it will be said that defined goals can be evaluated in a hard-headed and objective way, but not value as a characteristic of types or classes of action, or of situations, and not rights as moral demands attaching to human beings as human beings.

But this is to presume that some moral notions are better founded than others. There is no reason to claim, however, that some moral notions – duty or obligation, for example – are any more soundly based than any others. It was a 'hard-headed' philosopher of modern times, John Mackie (1917–81), who wrote: 'Moral entities – values or standards or whatever they may be – belong within human thinking and practice: they are either explicitly or implicitly posited, adopted or laid down. And the positing of rights is no more obscure or questionable than the positing of goals or obligations.'[10] So rights – and values, too – do not have to *come from* somewhere to become valid; their validity is, at least in part, a function of their being recognized as such.

In the end, I will have to return to the question of moral knowledge when I have secured a picture of the problem of knowledge on a wider and more general scale. But on the issue of rights as a base for practical engagement and social interaction, I can make a beginning, if I wish to do so, by initiating their recognition in my own treatment of people, and my own appraisal of the way things are.[11]

So what would be meant by saying that this would limit the validity of my judgements to me, or perhaps to my social class or group? I can understand this suggestion only as a personal declaration of my critic that he, or she, does not intend to join me in this recognition of rights, or this appreciation of value. I need not accept the charge that my moral position is relative or essentially personal, since such a charge could be made only from an external standpoint which is not available to human observers. We all (human beings, that is) stand on an equal footing here. Of course I am, I cannot but admit, the product of my own culture and tradition. But I have a mind, and a critical faculty, which I can apply as well as can my critics, to the moral standards I see around me – and, in the end, the position I choose to take is just that – a choice of position. And it is therefore without apology or qualification that I may decide to take as central just that right identified by Mackie as 'the right of persons progressively to choose how they shall live'.[12]

Applications: personal and domestic

This conclusion comes closer to another way in which Kant formulated his moral theory: it means treating persons as persons, as ends in themselves. Kant's phrase was to the effect that other people should be treated as equal lawmakers in a realm of ends. The first context in which I am likely to try out this or any other kind of principle of morality is the close family context – the familiar framework of intimate personal decisions.

Turning to this area, it is striking that many of the most difficult of these personal decisions – particularly those concerned with the beginning and end of life – are in fact posed in terms of rights. For example, decisions about whether, how and when to have children are increasingly being brought by medical and technical advances from the realm of the haphazard and ungovernable into the realm of choice; in these circumstances, the right of a woman to choose how she will use her body, the right of an unborn child to sustenance and safe delivery, the right of a father to his progeny, and the right of any particular child to a certain quality of life, are all factors which compete for priority in judgements about what to do in complex personal situations.

But rights feature, too, in the wider setting of personal relationships, with marriage as perhaps the paradigm case of promising. Of course, in the context of marriage, appeal to rights may be an indication that the relationship is already crumbling. The *values* of loyalty, support and good faith are of more long-term interest here. But rights do feature none the less, and children, for example, could be regarded as satellites of a marriage, having their own rights to stability and security. Here the question is whether there is any way – if this is desirable – to combine flexibility in relationships with stability, and with regard for these other obligations. Is this an area where there is a choice, or is later choice excluded by an initial but binding decision? Clearly, whatever conclusions I come to, they must be made in a social context in which both differing ways of expressing sexuality, and sexual relationships outside marriage, are widely accepted, and are reflected in a legal system which provides for easier divorce based on the fault of neither partner, as well as the removal of the ancient stigma of illegitimacy. This provides a setting in which old answers cannot be taken for granted, but where new answers must be personally supplied by me in the context of my own life.

Not just my *own* answers, though. One way or another, both male and female are compelled first and as a priority to settle their attitudes to these questions of personal and domestic relationships. Nevertheless, many of these questions may not impinge as decisions, but remain as undefined ambivalences of attitude, shelved for future resolution. One problem, however, has a special significance just because it cannot be shelved in this way. This is why, for those who face it, an abortion decision is the largest and most significant moral crisis faced in life.[13]

It presents itself as a decision because there is a time-factor built into the nature of the decision, which makes action unavoidable. This follows from the fact that biologically, of course, non-action is action and results in general in the birth of a living child – perhaps *the* most significant positive and creative production of anybody's life. And not merely a feminine act of creativity; for pregnancy and childbirth are also the only way that a man, vicariously, can produce a child. Action to forestall this end, if it is to be taken, must be taken urgently, firmly and – as the law presently stands – after much consideration and the taking of expert advice.

Here, then, is a moral decision which shows up the inadequacy of both a strictly utilitarian approach and also of an approach based on such principles or rules of conduct as 'Thou shalt not . . .' Recognition of the fact that here the rights of a potential child may be in conflict with the rights of an actual woman does not, of course, provide an answer either. And yet it provides a basis for clear-headed decision-making. There cannot be a guarantee that the decision taken will not be regretted. If a decision to abort later comes to be seen as wrong, then it is a more appalling wrong decision than any other that a woman – or indeed a man – may take. For the termination is the termination of the existence of one's own child, that which is biologically closest and most important to a person.

A wrong abortion decision, then, is not a trivial wrong decision. But, of course, circumstances may weigh; other values may be involved: the youth of the mother; conception following from criminal assault and rape: health factors of both mother and fetus – all these are standardly recognized as special factors, and there is no reason to suppose that where the law stops is the place also where all moral latitude would cease. Degree of development of the fetus, too, is a not unreasonable factor to take into account, and different moral attitudes may well be appropriate at different stages on the 'slippery slope' of this particular argument.[14]

Here, then, in these deep waters of personal life, and similarly in other areas where death, disability and illness may intrude, philosophical reflection and more considered decision-making may have a place as an alternative to unthinking and uncritical action and reaction.

It may take the form, say, of asking whether, in my relations with other people, the pursuit of personal gratification, pure hedonism, can provide a policy for behaviour. For the reasons already given, it is clear it will not. Using other people merely as a means to personal gratification is not a moral or a philosophical possibility. But what a policy of promoting happiness on a wider scale would entail in relation, for example, to the institution of marriage and family life, is so problematic that that, too, is hardly available as a solution to these pressing dilemmas of personal life.

The rigidity of a principle-based morality has already been noticed; in relation to the particular institution of marriage there is a special difficulty. Promises concerning personal relationships seem to involve a commitment to what is strictly outside the promis-or's control. After all, there are certain kinds of feeling which make a marriage relationship impossible, at least in respect to the sexual and emotional satisfaction which make of marriage more than an empty shell.

On a personal level, then, there may be conflict between the ideals of exclusivity and variety; of loyalty to one person, and of richness of personal relationships; there may be tension, too, between the ideals of permanence or long-term affection and the facts of change and the seemingly inevitable transitoriness of love. Some limited answer is possible, however, through the recognition of others as persons and the desire to respect their rights in the form of duties or obligations voluntarily accepted. This partial answer may be comp-lemented by the fact that I can also attach value to modes of behav-iour of my own that involve qualities such as kindness and sensitive understanding. And finally, in my struggle for a coherent moral per-spective, I find an indisputable further value in states of affairs free of misery and avoidable suffering for others.[15]

Applications: ethics and the workplace

But moral decision-making is not confined to the domestic sphere. It may play an important role in the workplace where, say, a decision whether or not to join a union, or whether or not to participate in a strike, may impinge as moral rather than merely practical questions. Perhaps, on the other hand, a problem of a different sort arises, as I come into possession of information about the practices of my employer, which poses a conflict of loyalty for me between what I owe to my employer and what I owe to the wider community.

What kind of moral questions are these? Once again, to describe the conflicts in terms of rights may clarify for me what is involved. The power of the unions and the power of multinational corporations affect the lives of individuals in ways that may create personal moral dilemmas for the nonconformist. If I have a right to join a union, do I also have a right *not* to join a union? Where compulsory union membership obtains, then others – maybe not I myself – may be prevented by their beliefs, perhaps only their beliefs in freedom of association, from gaining their livelihood by the skills in which they have been trained. On the face of it, there exists a right to be protected. But freedoms can sometimes be outweighed by other moral or political considerations. And other workers may advance an argument from injustice. Why should one person be allowed to profit from the work and sacrifice of others? Why accept a share in the benefits achieved by union bargaining whilst not contributing to the struggle? Although a straightforward appeal to fairness, this is an argument with utilitarian overtones. It presupposes that the people working in an industry or business are better off because of unions. But a wider utilitarian argument is possible and may also be used. This is the argument that national prosperity depends on industrial efficiency; that strong unions are needed for industrial efficiency and that compulsory union membership is necessary for strong unions, providing protection for individuals against pressure from employers.

At least some of these factual claims may be true. But, of course, the argument does not turn only on utility. Some may have religious objections to union membership; they may also have moral objections, in the sense that they believe people should not be forced by others to join an association against their will; and they may have political objections, in the sense of wishing to retain a personal right to complain – for instance, about conditions of work, or to take a decision whether or not to strike. In the latter case, a moral objection to striking may be involved, perhaps because the job in question is in the medical services or in a vital service where strikes cause suffering or danger to other, uninvolved people; and it may be this that accounts for the reluctance to transfer that ultimate right to the strike decision, through union membership, to a representative. Finally, a union may itself adopt policies, or support political causes or parties, with which the individual member disagrees. So, since these grounds of objection variously suggest circumstances in which a person may lose his or her job for religious, moral or political reasons, I may, as an individual considering these facts, be confronted with the need to take a moral stance immediately in relation to my own employment. The personal nature of these decisions is dramatically illustrated in the case of some strikes where bitter personal feelings are aroused. I may, for example, find a split within my own close family, or friends, as happened in the case of the miners' strike in Britain in 1984–5. A decision to cross or stand upon a picket-line is, or may be, an agonizing dilemma, a personal moral crossroad where the direction-signs are missing or obscured.[16]

The union issue is a matter, essentially, of the rights of the individual. But a workplace dilemma can arise, too, where the rights of people outside the organization or industry are concerned. I may find out that, say, safety procedures are being deliberately flouted, that environmental hazards are being concealed, or that potentially lethal corners are being cut in the manufacture of a commodity. There are many possible examples: the leakage of nuclear contamination; an escape of lethal dioxin; a car safety-device deliberately omitted as a result of a cost-benefit calculation where payment of compensation in the few unfortunate cases is deemed cheaper and therefore preferable to standard provision of the device. If I am a scientist or engineer working in these fields, then I am specially well qualified to recognize the lapse, if there is one, and may therefore consider myself specially responsible for opening up the issue.

Or, in public service, secrecy rules may be applied to cover the profiteering or inefficiency of politicians or public figures. If I were such a politician, I might wonder whether my role carried with it different moral responsibilities from those applying to individuals. Whatever the specific situation, if I am the only person in a position to blow the whistle to alert the unsuspecting public, I am likely to find myself in a situation of personal moral conflict – first of all one of loyalties: to the company or organization, to colleagues, to the wider public. If the decision is made in favour of the public, then the problem becomes no less a moral problem, but one of a more familiar sort: a problem of weighing the personal consequences, which may include a threat to career and livelihood, and deciding whether or not to face them; a problem of weakness or strength of will. But these calculations and considerations go beyond the personal. Whatever my decision, it is made in a social and political context. A framework of law provides the backdrop against which my moral perplexities are played out.[17]

So if I challenge the policy of a company or a branch of government – if I set my individual morality against a prevailing practice or received opinion – I can do it only because I have some wider judgement of the way things ought to be. My personal concern, in other words, becomes a wider, public concern. Morality merges into politics. My concern about myself becomes a concern about the rest of the world. And I can no longer, therefore, consider my own situation, my own answer to 'What shall I do?' outside this wider context.

Notes to Chapter 2

1. The reference is to the discussion in Book II of Plato's *Republic*, 359d–362d, which begins with the story of a shepherd, Gyges, who acquires a ring that can make him invisible. This gives him the option of doing wrong with impunity and raises the question: are the only sanctions against crime the ones society is able to impose, or can morality be justified *for the individual*?

2. Joseph Butler (1692–1752) who was Bishop of Bristol and later became Bishop of Durham argued in his *Fifteen Sermons* (in particular Sermon 11) that, whatever might be the case with hot, or impetuous, self-love, 'cool' self-love and virtue coincide.

3. For a penetrating discussion of psychological hedonism, see G. Ryle, *Dilemmas*, Chapter 4. Ryle exposes the fallacy of basing a theory of universal selfishness on the belief that if I want to have or to do something, then what I want is the *pleasure* of having or doing it. As Bishop Butler also pointed out, it is only by wanting things, bad or good, *for their own sakes*, that I *can* derive pleasure from them.

   Nevertheless, in the past philosophers – notably Plato and Aristotle – did assume that if a course of action was to be recommended, it was necessary to show that it would be for a person's own good, or at least not in conflict with it. The starker theory of psychological hedonism, particularly as put forward by the British philosopher Thomas Hobbes (1587–1678) gives a narrower materialistic slant to such an assumption, linking it to a theory of basic and simple psychological drives that leaves no room for altruistic action or action stemming from a purely moral motive. Psychological hedonism subsequently became one of the pillars of Bentham's form of utilitarianism, expressed in the claim that human beings are motivated solely by the desire to avoid pain and seek pleasure. Its other pillar, not easily reconciled with this, is that they ought to pursue the greatest happiness of the greatest number of people. While Mill and Bentham concurred in this opinion, they held differing views as to the nature of happiness. Unlike Bentham who took a quantitative view of pleasure, Mill believed that pleasures could be graded as 'higher' or 'lower', that human happiness and fulfilment is distinctively associated with the former, and that our obligation is to maximize the intellectual, cultural and spiritual pleasures rather than purely material ones.

4. J. Bentham, *Principles of Morals and Legislation*, Ch. I, sec. 11.
5. J. S. Mill, *Utilitarianism*, p. 4.
6. For a modern discussion of the pros and cons of utilitarianism, see J. J. C. Smart and B. Williams, *Utilitarianism: for and against*.
7. I. Kant, *Groundwork of the Metaphysic of Morals*, 402, in H. J. Paton, *The Moral Law*, p. 70. This was one of several formulations Kant offered of his famous 'categorical imperative'. Another formulation contained the injunction not to treat people solely as means but always to treat them as well as ends in themselves.
8. For a discussion of the need to have principles, but also to qualify them in particular circumstances, together with the problems this raises for moral education, see R. M. Hare, 'Principles', *Proceedings of the Aristotelian Society* Vol. 73, 1972–3.
9. Mary Midgley has discussed this in *Wickedness*. She argues there that it is only by recognizing the human capacity for wickedness (as opposed to explaining it away under such labels as social conditioning or mental illness) that there will be any hope of developing a realistic and effective morality.
10. J. Mackie, 'Can there be a right-based moral theory?', in J. Waldron (ed.), *Theories of Rights*, p. 171.
11. A. I. Melden has discussed the issue of rights in a personal and family context in *Rights and Persons*.
12. J. Mackie, op. cit., p. 175.
13. For a discussion of the centrality of the dilemma of choice in women's lives resulting from the possibility of effective birth-control and abortion, see Carol Gilligan's article, 'In a Different Voice: women's conceptions of self and morality'. She writes in relation to these situations: '[T]he relationships that have traditionally defined women's identities and framed their moral judgements no longer flow inevitably from their reproductive capacity but become matters of decision over which they have control' (p. 490).
14. There is a considerable philosophical literature on the subject of abortion. See in particular R. Hursthouse, *Beginning Lives*. For this and related issues, including a critical account of some contemporary feminist arguments, see Janet Radcliffe Richards, *The Sceptical Feminist*. The discussion on abortion is in Ch. 8.

15. For fuller discussion of moral aspects of marriage and sexual relation-ships, see Brenda Almond, *Moral Concerns*, Ch. 4. Questions raised there include: how far should the state, for social and economic reasons, impose through law the institutional structure of family relationships based on marriage as an exclusive sexual relationship? On a personal level, can one combine stability and flexibility in personal relationships?
16. R. M. Hare has written on the issue of compulsory union membership in 'A Kantian Utilitarian Approach', one of a collection of articles on these themes in *Moral Rights in the Workplace*, edited by Gertrude Ezorsky.
17. On these issues, see Sissela Bok: *Lying*, and also her later book *Secrets*. In the latter book, Bok examines the way in which international tensions, both military and commercial, have combined with technological advances to generate moves towards secrecy that threaten open societies. In both books she argues for truth-telling and open information in the main areas of public and private life.

Reading Guide to Chapter 2

The subject of this chapter has been moral philosophy. There are many good introductions to this subject, including:

J. Mackie: *Ethics*
P. Singer: *Practical Ethics*
W. Frankena: *Ethics*
A. MacIntyre: *A Short History of Ethics*

The issue of utilitarianism as a moral theory is best presented in: J. J. C. Smart and B. Williams: *Utilitarianism: for and against*, while a case for a morality of fixed principles is argued by E. Anscombe in an article entitled 'Modern Moral Philosophy', in her *Collected Philosophical Papers, Vol. III, Ethics, Religion and Politics*.

For discussion of specific contemporary moral issues see:

J. Glover: *Causing Death and Saving Lives*
R. Wasserstrom (ed.): *Today's Moral Problems*
J. Rachels: *Moral Problems*
S. Bok: *Lying*
    and *Secrets*
C. L. Reid (ed.): *Choice and Action*
B. Almond: *Moral Concerns*

Important modern works of broader scope include:

R. M. Hare: *Freedom and Reason*
    and *Moral Thinking*
J. Rawls: *A Theory of Justice*
A. I. Melden: *Rights and Persons*
B. Williams: *Ethics and the Limits of Philosophy*

A useful collection of papers is P. Foot (ed.): *Theories of Ethics*

Classical sources

Plato: *Dialogues*, particularly *Republic*, *Meno*, *Protagoras* and *Gorgias*
Aristotle: *Nichomachean Ethics*
Epictetus: *Moral Discourses*
Kant: *Groundwork of the Metaphysic of Morals*, best read in H. J. Paton: *The Moral Law*
Hume: *Enquiry Concerning the Principles of Morals*
J. S. Mill: *Utilitarianism*

3 Looking Outwards

> . . . although politics in itself is a difficult art, no art is
> required to combine it with morality. For as soon as the
> two come into conflict, morality can cut through the
> knot which politics cannot untie.
>
> — Immanuel Kant, Perpetual Peace

Making my own decisions, reflecting on my own life, are not, then,
things I can do in a vacuum. Instead, I am constantly brought up
against the boundaries of legal restraints, social pressures and political and economic structures. I may not choose conformity, but even
the nature of my nonconformity is set by this social context. In
addition, there seem to be things I want that I cannot achieve for
myself, not least the benefit that law brings by making other people's
actions predictable and acceptable to me.

As I have seen, when I reflect even on those personal and intimate
decisions which seem most in my hands – the domestic, the sexual,
the parental – I am bound to approach these decisions with prior
answers to another range of questions: for example, am I to regard
myself and others as atoms, units, isolated individuals colliding
with each other and then passing on to other collisions? Or do I
accept that human beings can fuse, pair, join together in groups and
associations which themselves constitute new entities or collectivi-
ties?

In the case of the simplest of associations – that between a man
and a woman – must I see this as providing the natural locus for child
raising – a process which can occupy the most active and productive
years of adult life? If I am inclined to a positive answer here, then my
answer (since what I have described is the basic social and economic

institution of the family) must have implications for my views on love and loyalty, hedonistic and short-term indulgence, sacrifice and self-denial. It will also require me to answer questions about the role of women and of men in society; about equality in employment; about social and financial provision for children, and about education. But more than this, I have to accept that my individual judgement may not always coincide with law and social expectation.

As for my workplace decisions, these even more conspicuously involve my reaction to, rather than action within, a political and legal framework. The great classical theorists of morality, Plato and Aristotle, were clear that individual morality opens up into a theory of citizenship. It is not surprising, then, that my own moral reflections, my preoccupation with the question of my strategy for living and my conception of morality, should require me also to ask: what is the right thing for my community to do? And since the organized community can support *its* answer to this question with sanctions of punishment and enforcement, law becomes the first focus of my expanding concern. I may ask: what is the relationship between law and morality? Does law reflect morality? Ought it to do so? Conversely, should morality be embodied or expressed in law? Should it at least conform to it?

The example of an abortion decision gave a particular point to these questions. If I regarded it as an individual decision, then this was to assume that either decision – for or against – would be legally permissible. But, of course, laws – and this one in particular – vary from place to place. So I can also ask: what *should* be the position of the law on this and other issues? If the law does not fit with my conception of how it ought to be, I may go on to ask: why should I obey the law as it is and as I find it? What obligation do I have to conform either to other people's expectations or to the requirements of the state?

Even if in general I wish to answer this in a positive way – I am for the most part happy to accept conformity – I am bound to set moral limits to this willingness. In other words, I must condone a certain amount of disorder even if I opt for law and order. There are those, I know, who would say that the law is to be obeyed simply because it is the law – but equating the 'might' of the law with the morally 'right' is simply incompatible with the honest and open search for truth that I have set as my goal.[1] It is incompatible, too, with the idea of reaching, for myself, a view as to what is right, and then taking responsibility for my own choices and decisions.

Law, conscience and toleration

One solution to these problems might be to try, at least in thought, to separate the areas of law and of morality. Perhaps, echoing a famous phrase in the Wolfenden Report of 1957, which made liberalizing recommendations regarding the law in England on homosexuality and prostitution, I decide that certain aspects of private life are just 'not the law's business'. Indeed, I would have to have a very intrusive view of law and social living if I were to deny this, since the denial would mean that every aspect of my life could be regarded as a potential canditate for regulation – even trivial and personal tastes and pursuits, private interests and preferences.

I cannot, then, take the law as beyond criticism. Others may wish to change the law and so may I. A conflict between law and morality will provide a good reason for such a change. A blatantly immoral law should not remain in force, I am prepared to claim, nor even an illiberal one, in which a practice is involved that seems a private matter. But if I decide in that way that the law should square with morality, whose morality is in question? Some, for example Lord Devlin, the British judge who has written in defence of the enforcement of morals, would say that not only is there a common morality within a community, but that this is the only sound basis of law.[2] This may be true. Perhaps there is a common morality which I can recognize as the dominant one in my society, but if it cuts across my own, I am confronted with the problems I have already considered. So the answer to my question – whose morality? – is the paradoxical-sounding one that it can only be my own.

But for law to square with morality and for law to impose it are two different things; and laws that are in existence for no other reason than to enforce morality – whether mine or a 'community view' – raise as many questions as immoral ones. Should there be laws against gambling, for example? Or against pornography? Should there be censorship of films and videotapes? In short, *should* morality be enforced by law? The answer to this can only be that a limit must be set to any such endeavour, not just by the recognition of individual rights but also by judging how the application of such values as freedom, toleration, equality and respect for the individual personality may work out in the case of each particular issue.

The problem of distinguishing the proper spheres of law and morality is most acute where the most difficult cases – abortion and euthanasia, for example – are concerned. In any case it is unlikely that there will ever be a perfect match between my notion of how the law should be and the way it in fact is. In the meantime, I have to accept as a fact the framework of law which I find in place. And yet I cannot abdicate my own responsibility to decide, if moral claims conflict with legal ones as they may do in some extreme situations, whether to follow these and my conscience, or to do what is expected of me. And at a certain level, law itself supports me in this. Watergate, My Lai and Nuremberg are all names which provide a reminder that individuals have, after the event, been held legally as well as morally responsible for actions which were judged to offend against a higher morality, even if set in some kind of context of authority or legality at the time.

This may be less anarchic in practice than it sounds in theory. Accepting that it might in certain circumstances be right to break the law is not an argument for a *policy* of selective obedience to the law. I can imagine three kinds of situation where the case for disobedience would be strong:

1. Where what is forbidden is an essential aspect of a person's nature and personality – for example, homosexuality where this is a criminal offence.
2. Where the law itself is morally objectionable – for example, sitting in the part of a bus reserved for another race, where the law enforces racial segregation.
3. Where disobedience to the law is incidental to some other action someone wants to take, possibly for strong moral reasons – for example, camping at Greenham Common in the hope of preventing the deployment of Cruise missiles.

There are, of course, other even more controversial cases where the issue of law-breaking might arise: for example, where protest itself has been made illegal; or where the authority of the law-makers is disputed; or in circumstances, perhaps, where a separatist organization aims to institute a break-away government expressive of a particular culture, language and race.

Even the first three cases listed, though, seem to undermine my earliest presumptions about law, disorder and the place of conscience, if initially I was inclined to assume that I must work within (rather than against) social and legal constraints. There are many cases of civil disobedience which have, retrospectively, won the respect and admiration even of those against whom they were directed: Gandhi's passive resistance, which contributed ultimately to the independence of India; the burning of draft-cards in the United States, which expressed a widespread demand that US involvement in Vietnam be brought to an end; and, in the southern states of America, the positive breaking of laws about racial segregation in the 1960s, which substantially altered the climate of thought for the next generation.

One thing these particular examples have in common, however, is that, if they involved violence to others, this was not as a matter of policy. Perhaps, then, I may endorse *non-violent* protest as an uncontroversial way in which my own moral perspective may be retained and expressed in a climate of law and opinion which runs counter to it?

But there are two ways in which I may find this inadequate as a general solution to problems of law and disorder, protest and dissent. First, such protest is not always successful. Lying down in front of tanks is effective only if there is a sufficient degree of humanity in those manning them, or those giving orders, for the tanks to roll to a stop. But not all political opponents count human life as valuable as this. And a hunger strike is effective only against people who would regard the death of a hunger-striker with concern and whose system of government is open enough for public information about it to be released; for many regimes, however, human life is cheap and people may starve themselves to death in prison without fanfare. What is more, where political will is strong, peaceful protest will not always alter policies: it is true that the Vietnam War was brought to an end; not true, though, that Cruise missiles were excluded from Britain and other parts of Western Europe as a result of local opposition, nor that the deaths of hunger-strikers brought significant changes in British policy in Northern Ireland.

Secondly, even peaceful protest forces confrontation between protesters and the representatives of legal authority, often the civil police. Clearly, I must weigh the importance of the cause for which I make my protest against the damage I do to the fabric of law and order – a structure which, I have already acknowledged, provides the support and underpinning of my existence as a choosing, acting individual.

But if the issue is vital, and the end cannot be achieved by other means? Or if conformity to the law makes my life and existence intolerable by demanding, even where other people's interests are scarcely involved, that I suppress my deepest urges and abandon all hope of self-fulfilment? Even in these circumstances, the moral restraints I have recognized as affecting my own private life may make me unwilling to move from peaceful to violent protest, from placards to bombs, from political argument to terrorism. For these are activities I cannot engage in without transgressing the rights of others, too, to enjoy the conditions necessary for an unimpeded life. A passing stranger torn apart by a bomb, a traveller or embassy employee held hostage against the actions of governments – these are inevitably being deprived of the very things I claim against others for myself. So if such values as humanity or fellow-feeling do not restrain me, I must at least contemplate the stark plea of other people's rights.

Consideration of my own position, then, in respect of laws as they are and as I find them, suggests that, since I must ultimately retain a right to moral judgement, I have also a limited right to frugally and discriminatingly exercised civil disobedience, so long as this remains short of gratuitous invasion of the rights of others to life, happiness and health.[3]

But when I consider my attitude to the actions and behaviour of others, then I find a different issue engaging my attention. This is the issue of toleration. In considering my own position, I have recognized my own prior interest in a secure framework of conformity to the law on the part of other people; if I find myself surrounded by dissent and nonconformity, I may be unable to pursue my own goals and aspirations without hindrance. As a minimum, I may find the chosen life-styles of others offensive or alarming.

The kind of limits to protest which I have just defined for myself, will, then, be what I will demand of others, whatever their degree of moral conviction and no matter how important, in their own eyes, they take their cause to be. Where the dissent of others is concerned, two attitudes are possible: either I may decide that this is a case where the law should indeed be changed (for example, that homosexuality should be decriminalized) or I may believe that the case is not one for toleration, and thus that the law as it stands should be enforced.

But defining the limits of toleration is no easy matter. Two cases which press against these limits might be these: (i) the case of people who hold racist beliefs and wish to promote them; (ii) the case of groups who believe in the subservience of women and adopt educational strategies and religious or cultural practices which it is difficult or impossible for individual women to resist. Are these cases for toleration, or cases for limiting by law what can rightly not be tolerated? The British philosopher John Stuart Mill, in his classic defence of toleration *On Liberty*,[4] argued that a clear line could be drawn in answering such questions between the parts of a person's conduct that concern or affect only that person, and those which also affect others. Beliefs and opinions belong to the first category; actions against members of a race or a whole sex belong to the second. But the problem with these two particular cases lies in deciding how far beliefs and opinions in such matters can be separated from actions. If laws relating to *actions* are called for by the recognition of rights, then perhaps laws against the expression of the *opinions* which gave rise to the actions would be appropriate, too.

Here it seems that there is no alternative but to return to my own starting point, the philosophical commitment to open discussion and freedom of thought. In doing this I see that acting and thinking are not totally separable and unrelated; rather, they shade into each other. There is, in fact, a continuum stretching from mere opinion, through the expression of opinion, proselytizing for an opinion, inciting to action, and finally to action itself. Drawing a line somewhere on this continuum will obviously not be easy, and where it *is* to be drawn may vary from case to case. But my presumption must be in favour of toleration where that end of the continuum is concerned that represents belief and discussion: only this is consistent both with my starting point and with my chosen method of procedure. But my recognition of other people's rights, and of the need for those who otherwise may be defenceless to be protected by law and social institutions, will justify the outlawing of action and incitement to action which poses a threat to those rights.

At this point, however, I recognize that my judgements are becoming judgements, not about what I myself should do, but about what the law should be. And to reflect on what the law should be, to campaign perhaps that existing laws should be changed or new ones brought in, is to engage in a well-known and historic art: the art of politics. At this point, I have to recognize that my personal moral concern has broadened into political concern – that is, a concern that my country or government should reflect in broad outline the moral outlook I have arrived at as an individual.

Law, morality and the art of politics

My reflections on protest, dissent and nonconformity suggested a difference in the way in which the authorities in any particular country might respond to them; indeed, looking about the contemporary world, it would not be difficult to distinguish a spectrum of political practices based on the degree of responsiveness of governments to protest. Protest in a liberal democracy might therefore seem to raise different questions, differently answered, from protest under a totalitarian regime, or under a regime which is itself illegal or self-imposed, the result of a military coup or of corruption and chicanery.

Seeing that my moral evaluation of governments may vary, I realize that I expect that governments, too, should operate within moral limits, that they should be regarded as being under the same kind of principles of restraint as individuals, especially given their vastly greater powers and opportunities. So the kind of reasons that operated against terrorism for the individual operate against the use of arbitrary imprisonment, torture, summary execution and the abuse of human rights by governments.

This is to suggest that there is a relationship between the individual and the state in which the power of the one must in some way be balanced by the claims of the other. I know that the nature of this relationship, and the justification of the obedience exacted of the individual to the demands of the state, have been the focus of some of the great classics of political philosophy, including Plato's *Republic*, Hobbes' *Leviathan* (1651), Locke's *Second Treatise of Government* (1690) and Rousseau's *Social Contract* (1762).

One answer which was common to all these writers was that the obligation of individuals to obey must in some way or other be shown to follow from their own agreement or consent – the theory of the social contract. The idea of political power as something which is simply imposed on people is no answer to the philosophical issue of obligation or justification. These writers varied as regards the manner and nature of the consent involved; Plato, for example, painted a relatively simple picture in *Republic*, Book II, of men coming together to fulfil specialist functions and profit from exchange and barter. For Thomas Hobbes, civil society was a matter of a once-and-for-all surrender of one's political will to an absolute sovereign, limited only by the freedom to resist an order for one's own death. For John Locke (1632–1704), the agreement was a continuing tacit agreement signalled by a person's willingness to stay within the borders of his country of birth. While Jean-Jacques Rousseau's (1712–78) social contract was a matter of the imposition of a consensus (the General Will) to which an individual might be deemed as contributing through a system of majority voting – an outcome which, Rousseau held, revealed what the individual *really* wanted, as opposed to what he merely *thought* he wanted.

But today's individual can have little effect on policy within the borders of a single country; nor can individuals readily move away from the jurisdiction of the country in which they are born, and then only into that of another which might be equally objectionable to them. And in any case, technology has turned the world, in a popular phrase, into a global village in which the maladministration of one nation is the practical problem of another.

Politics: the environmental dimension

This feature of the interdependence of nations is particularly striking where environmental issues are concerned. For example, an accident at Chernobyl, in Russia, sent radioactive fallout over most of Europe; trees die in Scandinavia as a result of industrial processes in other parts of Europe; the Mediterranean receives the effluent (detergents, pesticides, oil and chemicals, as well as sewage) of sixteen surrounding countries until these countries are forced into concerted action to preserve it as a living sea; French rivers are polluted as a result of German chemical processes; at Bhopal in India, people died from a leak resulting from the local manufacture of a chemical marketed by a multinational company; and a single nation may, by its uncontrolled policies, hunt or fish a species to extinction. These problems could in general be summed up as problems of pollution and problems of depletion of resources, including energy-resources.

What should be my reaction to such facts, and to such reports as that of the Club of Rome, which used the title *The Limits to Growth*[5] to underline its projections of future disaster if current trends continue unchecked? While some would dismiss such reports as alarmist, their views have to be set against the fact that the United Nations has regarded the issues as being serious enough to justify setting up a number of environment-monitoring agencies. And, indeed, it seems clear that it is not possible for individual nations to tackle piecemeal technical problems which are problems for the whole planet.

Surveying these facts, I may conclude that we – human beings, that is – will need, in the end, to recognize the finitude of the earth's resources and to accept whatever turn out to be the natural limits to growth. As a resident of a western industrialized nation, I may query the political goals of unrestrained expansion and growth. I will also want to consider whether these problems of ecology and environment are likely, in the end, to be controlled only by international political agencies which could monitor global hazards on a global scale, enforcing global remedies.

But some philosophers have argued that such a strategy is inconsistent with individual freedom, and also that environmental concern is, moreover, a luxury of the wealthy nations at the expense of the poor. The only possible answer to the first objection is that the basic requirements of the individual are, first of all, protection of health and life and, secondly, freedom to choose which life- and health-affecting hazards to accept and which to reject. For example, people's liberty is restricted if they are forced to ingest chemicals along with ordinary foods as a result of farming and marketing practices over which they have no control. Personal freedom is also affected if the river on which a community depends is destroyed by the effects of industrial processes. And the autonomy of future generations of individuals is significantly endangered if, in greedy pursuit of energy, this generation recklessly stockpiles dangerous radioactive waste with a 'life' of tens of thousands of years. As regards the second objection, it is only possible to say that the environment is a common heritage, so that a threat to one is a threat to all, and also that many environmental gains can be achieved only by the acceptance of less profligate ways of living by the wealthier nations.[6]

Poverty and plenty

But consideration of the environmental links between nations makes it clear that not all nations are on an equal footing in these matters. The wealth of the world is vastly unequally owned, with power and influence correspondingly disproportionate. Some people must live out their lives on the brink of starvation, or indeed die in massive droughts and famines; while others use enormous resources to replace worn hearts, lungs or defective organs. In the West, the doctrine of the sanctity of life is applied to keeping alive those whose prognosis is tragic. Elsewhere, young and middle-aged alike are swept out of existence by avoidable disease and malnutrition. A great gulf divides the developed and industrialized nations, largely from the northern hemisphere, and the underdeveloped and developing countries, largely of the southern hemisphere, where overpopulation, poverty and malnutrition are endemic problems, and nations are subject to periodic droughts and cycles of natural disasters.

Are these matters of economics? Or of politics? It seems that only political will could apply economic solutions. That there is an obligation to seek for solutions is a matter of common agreement. Some contemporary philosophers have argued that an obligation to tackle these problems can be based on utilitarian ethical foundations – there is a need to minimize pain and suffering. This is an effective argument, but the argument from rights is no less strong. And one problem with the utilitarian position is that it can, of its nature, provide no upper limits to what it might be our duty to do. Nevertheless, the philosopher Peter Singer (b. 1946) has developed a strong moral argument to the effect that individuals in wealthy countries ought to use their income to reduce absolute poverty in poorer countries, since they can, in general, do this without sacrificing anything of moral significance. If taken seriously, Singer's argument demands considerable sacrifice of comfort, since the yardstick of Third World need is a stringent one.[7]

The moral case for generosity is, then, at least as strong as a case based on moral claims or rights, although there may be pragmatic economic argument about its effects which will have to enter into utilitarian calculation. But in any case, I must ask myself whether this is the best, or the only, way for an individual to contribute to the solution of these problems. Is individual effort better directed, I wonder, to securing political solutions of a different kind to problems which are global and international? This is a question that strikes me with even more force in relation to one further range of problems of dominating significance: those connected with nuclear power and the threat of war, both conventional and nuclear.

The nuclear issue and the threat of war

Overlying all other problems, then, and dwarfing them in significance, is the shadow and the threat of nuclear war, together with the inextricably related issue of the development of nuclear energy. The non-proliferation of nuclear weapons (agreed with unsurprising unanimity by those nations already in possession of them to be a desirable objective) is not really compatible with expanding technical knowledge and expertise in the development of peaceful uses of nuclear energy, since the same knowledge and facilities that contribute to uses of nuclear energy for peace could be converted to uses for war. This adds a new dimension to a problem which is as old as mankind, the problem of war.

Can war ever be justified? There is a long tradition of theorizing about the 'just war'. Aggressive war has been outlawed by some international agreements, but war in self-defence is usually recognized as morally justified. Nevertheless, many innocent people will die if a nation defends itself, including its own nationals, so that a case could be made for avoiding even a war of self-defence if causing the death of innocent people were taken as invariably and absolutely wrong.

In the past, the aim for which a war was fought has been seen as justifying it: to free slaves, for example, or to protect a small nation from an aggressive invader or, more controversially, to free a population from a despotic tyranny. But war must be the bluntest of instruments for such purposes, and contemporary conditions make the possibility of applying economic or diplomatic pressure in effect an alternative and less painful weapon for use in this kind of cause.

Today's debates are conducted, though, less in terms of war than in those of deterrence. So the question is whether the morality of deterrence is different from the morality of war itself. This is a particularly potent question where nuclear weapons are concerned, where carrying out the threat would involve the slaughter and maiming of many innocent people: babies, children, old people, pregnant women, the sick in hospital, political campaigners for peace, as well as, through radiation, future as yet unborn people. Beyond this, the ultimate threat in a nuclear exchange is the doomsday threat of mutual total destruction. Surely, I may say, since it would be wrong to do this – to launch such retaliation – it must be wrong to threaten to do it.[8]

Against this has to be set the fact that people (would-be aggressors, for example) are more inclined to do what they can do with impunity and to avoid what will have undesirable consequences for themselves; and secondly, that while everything is lost if a threat must be carried through, nevertheless if the danger is appalling enough, it may be worth the risk of using a dangerous threat to avert it. The spread of nuclear weapons among those who may not make such rational assessments is nevertheless a matter for concern. Already, irresponsible people hold horrific weapons of war in their hands –

and in this case, the measure of 'irresponsibility' is that one uses them. A prime recent example has been the repeated reports of the gassing of human beings like insects in the Iran–Iraq war. So for the nuclear question as well as for other important issues, the preservation of peace is the indisputable requirement, and the question of how this is to be achieved has indisputable priority.

Clearly no single government can guarantee such a goal. For the governments of the world exist in what Hobbes described as a 'state of nature'. And Hobbes depicted the existence of individuals, as long as they were in that condition, – as a war 'of every man, against every man' and 'the life of man, solitary, poore, nasty, brutish and short'.[9] If such a situation is to be averted amongst the nations of the world and some equivalent of a social contract reached, then it seems that an international political entity must be the solution. In the present century, both the League of Nations and its successor, the United Nations, were set up with this aim; but neither could be said to have succeeded in meeting all the aspirations of the originators. Any bureaucratic organization, and not least an international one, is subject to perversion of purpose by the natural corruption of human beings – wheeler-dealing, fixing, a willingness to assert the morally absurd, the visibly false. No organization can be better than its officials, and people with a sense of moral purpose seldom progress in bureaucratic structures. If world-scale political action, no matter how desirable, is not able to provide an immediate solution to problems which cannot be deferred, then the political question is: what is to be done, and who should do it?

Individuals, charities, governments and world agencies

Governments already exist; therefore their role and contribution can, to some extent, be taken for granted. But whatever form it takes – aid to drought-stricken areas, loans and technical assistance, or disarmament negotiations and peace-keeping activities – it must be accepted that all this will be within the limits of their structure: their need to be responsive to electorates; to maximize the standard of living of their own nation; to protect their own inhabitants. And to do all this subject to managerial, electoral and bureaucratic constraints.

For achievable results, then, I may look again at the possible contribution of the individual outside the area of conventional politics. This, too, is bound to be limited, but nevertheless it is significant that *some* rare individuals *have* made a discernible impact on world events and on some at least of the problems mentioned. These include, to make an arbitrary list:

- the founder of Amnesty International, Peter Benenson;

- Mother Teresa of Calcutta;

- the founder of Greenpeace, and those individual members of that organization who deliberately place themselves at risk in nuclear test-zones or where radioactive or noxious emissions are suspected;

- the singer Bob Geldof, who originated Live Aid and its successor, Sport Aid.

The organizations mentioned here could be regarded as maverick, free-floating organizations, but nevertheless as a new phenomenon in the world with some influence over the actual course of events. Amnesty International's reports on torture and political persecution are, at a minimum, taken with some seriousness by some governments. Greenpeace has raised the level of public awareness of the activities of governments and commercial organizations in relation to environmental matters. Individual activists have made such issues as missile deployment or animal experimentation live questions rather than accepted routine. The organizations involved resemble on the one hand charities of the more established kind; on the other, pressure groups or purely campaigning organizations.

Apart from these, two other groupings provide a means whereby an individual may, whether as volunteer or employee, make a personal contribution in some of these areas: these are, first, the major charities, now powerful and institutionalized, which are heavily involved in problems of poverty, hunger, crisis and emergency; and secondly, the international agencies set up under the United Nations to cover special needs and problems. I need not assume, then, the complete ineffectiveness of individual effort, particularly if channelled through such sources. But how far, I wonder, should I personally see solutions to such problems as being in my own hands, and how far look to others or to a new international order?

In attempting to answer this question, I am struck by a distinctive aspect of the contemporary shape of politics. This is the way in which, while problems have broadened by becoming internationalized, political action has narrowed, flowing into single-issue groupings: animal welfare; feminism; black rights; national liberation movements; nuclear disarmament. It is true that there is a broad grouping of attitudes on these matters that coincides with the old party divisions of left and right; but this agreement on *image* covers a good deal of internal disagreement on *content*. In any case, since governments are based on parties, whether a single party or more, it is difficult for individuals to express a political wish, through conventional structures, for anything other than a package-deal, parts of which will be bound to be unacceptable to them. There is, in other words, both a formal face of politics in which compromise on issues is a way of life, and a new, informal face of politics consisting of single-issue groupings within which total commitment is the badge of membership.

Philosophy is influenced by this pattern, with both direct discussion of particular issues[10] and, at the same time, a broader shape of political theorizing which interprets for today traditional debates about political obligation. It is to this broader shape that I must turn if I am to resolve any further the question of my own political commitment.

Philosophical perspectives on politics

Political philosophy in the past has been centrally concerned with the issue of coercion: the individual person's obligation to obey, and the state's right to enforce compliance. The main contemporary currents of political thought fall on a spectrum from left to right in terms of their contribution to this debate. The extremes are marked by philosophers of the New Right in America, Britain, Australia and France, and by radical movements of the left, mainly in Western Europe, which take their inspiration from Marx, and particularly the young Marx. At the same time, the older liberalism, which has its roots in the tradition associated with J. S. Mill, continues to influence political thought.

Anarchy, State and Utopia,[11] by the contemporary American philosopher Robert Nozick (b. 1938), represents that view from the Right which recommends minimal state interference in the life of the individual. Nozick argues for the justification of what has been called a 'night-watchman' or minimal state – one limited to the narrow functions of protection for the individual against force, theft and fraud, and to the enforcement of contracts. In particular he argues that the state should not use its coercive apparatus for welfare – that is, to get some citizens to help others – and also that the state should not act paternalistically: it should not prohibit activities for people's own good. A basic element in Nozick's argument is the notion of entitlement as a principle of distribution. People who favour a welfare state, he argues, are regarding other people's assets, including their skills and talents, as belonging to a common pool, and they look for ways to distribute the benefits from these assets (as well as property more conventionally understood) on the basis of such principles as future utility, or equality. Alternatively, they might favour principles such as moral merit or usefulness to society. But Nozick's entitlement principle resembles none of these. It looks backward at how a right came into being rather than forward to how a good might be distributed. It is the reverse of Marx's dictum 'To each according to his needs' and might be described, by contrast, as 'To each his own'. It includes the view, for example, that taxation is slavery, or at least forced labour.

Such libertarian views (which are also associated with the work of Milton Friedman (b. 1912) and F. A. Hayek (b. 1899) – two economists whose ideas have been influential in promoting the tax-reducing, inflation-curbing policies of monetarist governments in America, Britain and Australia) start from a primary interest in the possession and management of property. Although primarily economic, these views may have implications for war and defence policy as well. One of the French '*nouveaux philosophes*', André Glucksmann (b. 1937), defends the French nuclear deterrent in impassioned terms,[12] while the Freedom Association in Britain surprisingly makes 'defence against the Queen's enemies' its first priority, taking precedence over any personal and individual liberties.

This form of libertarianism may be uneasily bound together with moral authoritarianism and support for the traditional family struc- ture as a replacement for the welfare functions of the modern state. There is another form of libertarianism, though, more solidly rooted in individual freedom, which differs from this in being open not only to men, but also to individualistically minded women. (For this recent variety seems, at least tacitly, to require that women resume the function recently taken over by the welfare state, by returning (whether they like it or not) to a domestic role which covers the care of the young, the ill or disabled and the aged.) This other form of libertarianism is closer to classical liberalism, and is libertarianism tempered by the humanitarianism that Mill found consistent with his own defence of the individual. In some ways this form of liberalism finds a meeting point with the humanistic Left which may itself be liberal in the sense of rejecting social and political curbs on individual action.

Representative of this sort of view is the political philosophy put forward by Antonio Gramsci (1891–1937) and his followers. It is an undogmatic and humanistically orientated form of western Marxism, one version of which has emerged as Euro-communism; and it could be summed up in Gramsci's demand (made in 1917) for a revolution 'against Capital', that is, against the belief that human action is insignificant, and against the idea that, in accordance with the historical, economic and social laws set out by Karl Marx (1818–83) in *Das Kapital*, capitalism would collapse through its internal contradictions, to be succeeded by a classless communistic society. The humanistic view, which emphasizes Marx's debt to Hegel (1770–1831), is associated particularly with the work of the Frankfurt School.[13]

Gramsci's rejection of historical determinism led him to advocate a 'philosophy of praxis' – he believed, that is, that philosophy should provide a way of interpreting the world that can be applied in practi- cal activity – which accords with another famous dictum of Marx in his *Theses on Feuerbach*: 'So far philosophers have only interpreted the world: the point, however, is to change it.'

Gramsci occupies an unusual position in relation to the extremes of right and left as they have been manifested in the present century. Living in Italy at a time when Mussolini and the Fascists were in power, he saw fascism as the 'illegal aspect of capitalist violence' – the only way that capitalists could preserve their economic system after the First World War. At the same time he regarded the Russian Revolution as practical evidence of human beings' control over their own destinies – an essentially libertarian phenomenon. Gramsci's Marxism then, propounded as it was in a series of notebooks written over years in a Fascist prison, is anti-totalitarian and his criticism of fascism is implicitly also a condemnation of Stalinism.[14]

I find the contemporary philosophical spectrum of views on the Left represented by a wide variety of Marxist, neo-Marxist and radical publications and movements,[15] and the liberal view more narrowly represented by, for example, Isaiah Berlin's (b. 1909) 'Two Concepts of Liberty',[16] and by the widely influential book in the liberal tradition by the contemporary American philosopher John Rawls (b. 1921), *A Theory of Justice*, which represents a modern version of the social contract theory.[17]

These last, in particular, suggest to me that what is common to various forms of philosophical liberalism is concern with a range of principles, beginning with those of personal liberty and toleration, but including also opposition to arbitrary government on the one hand, and rule by mere majority-*diktat* on the other – in other words, commitment to the rule of law. Personal liberty here includes such specific freedoms as those of thought, speech, publication and religion. There is a natural association between advocating freedom and respecting equality. So liberalism may also include a commitment to equality, as, for example, it does in Rawls's theory. Hence its sensitivity to the rights of minorities and of women and children. It is also characteristic of a liberal approach that it assumes politics to be a matter of trial and error – a pragmatic view of politics as piecemeal engineering rather than as Utopian reconstruction put forward by Karl Popper (b. 1902) in *The Poverty of Historicism*.

Rawls's theory, while it fits within this tradition and approach, is worked out from first principles. Rawls derives rules for ordering social life from a thought-experiment in which members of a society decide on basic moral principles for organizing their life from behind a 'veil of ignorance'. This protects them from knowledge of their own position in society, as well as their own competences and propensities. These conditions – called by Rawls the 'original position' – are what are necessary to secure impartiality of judge-ment, if it is assumed that the participants in the agreement are both rational and self-interested. In Rawls's 'general conception' there is, subject to the priority of freedom, a presumption in favour of the equal distribution of social goods. An unequal distribution would be acceptable only if it were to improve the position of the worst-off in society. This could be the case if, for example, great disparities of wealth or privilege were instrumental in raising the standard of liv-ing of a society beyond what it would be if equality were the rule.

This is a detailed working-out of a philosophical argument for a liberal state well to the left of Nozick's, but nevertheless not incom-patible with a free-enterprise system like that of modern America – provided, that is, that inequalities do as a matter of fact work in favour of the underprivileged.

Berlin's defence of liberalism is not dependent on any such factual assumptions. Delivered in Oxford in 1958, Berlin's 'Two Concepts of Liberty' sets out two conceptions of liberty, one negative, the other positive. The first answers the question: 'What is the area within which a person should be left to do or be what he wants to do or be?'; while the second, positive, sense answers the question: 'Who, or what, is the source of control or interference?' The first view is consciously derived from Mill, and Berlin argues that it is Mill's individualistic conception of man that lies behind '. . . every plea for civil liberties and individual rights, every protest against exploi-tation and humiliation, against the encroachment of public auth-ority, or the mass hypnosis of custom or organized propaganda'. On the other hand, Berlin claims, the positive conception is at the heart of all those political theories of self-realization which operate through 'magical transformation' or 'sleight of hand' to turn domi-nation into liberty, 'Enough manipulation with the definitions of man, and freedom can be made to mean whatever the manipulator wishes.' At the heart of Marxism and other totalitarian creeds, Berlin writes, is the view that knowledge liberates. We will cease to want what we see to be impossible or unattainable. But Berlin himself believes in a pluralism of values which, even if they are not necess-arily all achievable together and even if they turn out in the end to be a minority commitment, are nevertheless worth pursuing.

Berlin's reference to manipulation and sleight of hand is a

reminder that in these matters appearances may be deceptive. There is a problem about determining what truth is in a political context. And here the thought that politicians, if not political parties, may have a vested interest in concealing the true nature of issues takes on a special significance. I realize that, in assessing the issues and deciding on my own position, I am dependent on truth as it reaches me through media – the press, radio, television – which may be under the control, direct or indirect, of the very people whose position and views I am trying to assess. If any single conviction has emerged from my reflections on my own position in relation to the world and to world issues, it is the conviction that I must be left free, particularly in the matter of my judgement. But if I am to be free in my judgement – if I am not to be manipulated by others – then I must have access to information and argument which is accurate, undistorted and fair. I must next consider, then, what these requirements amount to. Are there ways of recognizing bad arguments and misleading information and, if so, can they be formulated?

Notes to Chapter 3

1. For the debate about legal positivism, see H. L. A. Hart, *The Concept of Law*, Chs. 8 and 9, and R. Dworkin, 'Is law a system of rules?', in R. M. Dworkin (ed.), *The Philosophy of Law*, Ch. 7. Jeremy Bentham, who rejected the notion of natural rights, is associated with the idea of law as command, which is distinctive of the legal positivist position. Legal positivism is the view that certain social facts (the will of the people, for example, or the commands of a ruler) determine what the law is. Nevertheless, many positivists, including Bentham himself as well as his follower John Austin (1790–1859), have held that the law is *not* always as it ought to be. Hans Kelsen (1881–1973) reiterated the positivist view that law and morality are separate spheres.

2. P. Devlin, *The Enforcement of Morals*. Lord Devlin's lecture was a reaction to the Wolfenden Report which, in recommending the liberalization of laws concerning homosexuality and prostitution, initiated a continuing debate about morality, particularly sexual morality, and the law.

3. For discussion of the issue of civil disobedience, see R. Dworkin, *Taking Rights Seriously*, Ch. 8.

4. J. S. Mill, *On Liberty* (first published 1859). An earlier classic statement of the case for toleration of opinion is contained in Locke's *Letters on Toleration* (1688 and following). The principle of religious toleration

was given expression with some poignancy (since they themselves were sometimes victims of its absence) by various religious leaders and philosophers in seventeenth- and eighteenth-century Europe, during times of religious upheaval and persecution. The best known of these advocates of toleration is probably Pierre Bayle (1647–1706). For an account of the history of ideas on toleration, see H. Kamen, *The Rise of Toleration*.

5. D. H. Meadows *et al.*, *The Limits to Growth*.

6. The ethical and political issues of environment and ecology are discussed by H. J. McCloskey in *Ecological Ethics and Politics*. Some of these issues are also discussed in R. Elliot and A. Gare (eds.), *Environmental Philosophy*. The broader issue of man's place in nature is the subject of John Passmore's *Man and his Place in Nature*, while particular philosophical interest in animal rights is reflected in the writings of Peter Singer. It is striking that all these authors are working in Australia, where interest in environmental philosophy is particularly strong.

7. Singer's position is set out in *Practical Ethics* and in his article 'Famine, Affluence and Morality'. While Singer represents a utilitarian ethical position on these matters, Onora O'Neill, in her book *Faces of Hunger*, discusses the issues of poverty and famine from a Kantian perspective.

8. This argument is the subject of an article by S. I. Benn, 'Deterrence or Appeasement? or, On Trying to be Rational about Nuclear War'. The issue of war is also discussed in R. Wasserstrom (ed.), *War and Morality*, and in R. Philips, *War and Justice*.

9. T. Hobbes, *Leviathan*, ed. C. B. MacPherson, Part 1, Ch. 13, pp. 185–6.

10. See, for example, such journals as *Philosophy and Public Affairs*, *Journal of Applied Philosophy* and *Ethics*, as well as discussions in journals covering a wider range of topics such as *Philosophy*, the journal of the Royal Institute of Philosophy.

11. R. Nozick, *Anarchy, State and Utopia*. With publication of this book, Robert Nozick, a Harvard philosopher and younger colleague of Rawls, offered a philosophical underpinning to a new libertarian trend in political thought.

12. See André Glucksmann, *La Force du Vertige*. Glucksmann writes: 'L'homme de paix ne serait pas nucléairement armé s'il était l'homme de la paix à tout prix; l'homme de guerre ne peut vouloir les guerres à n'importe quel coût s'il côtoie un adversaire comme lui capable du Grand Jeu.' ['The man of peace would not have nuclear arms if he was a man of peace-at-any-price; the man of war cannot want wars irrespective of cost if he encounters an adversary as capable as himself of Staking his All.']

Glucksmann is one of a group of French anti-Marxist philosophers who came to prominence in the mid-1970s. He and other 'nouveaux philosophes' see the main threat to freedom in Soviet Russian influence, to which they would wish to offer a distinctive French response.

13. Representatives of the Frankfurt School include M. Horkheimer (1895–1973), T. W. Adorno (1903–69), H. Marcuse (1898–1979) and J. Habermas (b. 1929).
14. For this view, see A. Sassoon, *Gramsci's Politics*. Gramsci's own writings are best read in A. Gramsci, *Prison Notebooks*.
15. In particular, the journal *Radical Philosophy*, a selection from which is published in *The Radical Philosophy Reader*, edited by R. Osborne and R. Edgley.
16. I. Berlin, 'Two Concepts of Liberty', in *Four Essays on Liberty*. Berlin's short essay, first delivered as an inaugural lecture at the University of Oxford in 1958, has had an influence disproportionate to its length. It captures for contemporary readers something of the high traditions and essence of liberalism.
17. J. Rawls, *A Theory of Justice*. Rawls's lengthy treatise was acknowledged as a major and seminal contribution to a range of areas of political and social theory almost as soon as it appeared in 1971. It offers a rich field for reflection and discussion to philosophers of law, economists, moral philosophers and social theorists.

Reading Guide to Chapter 3

This chapter is about political philosophy. A good way to begin reading contemporary work in political philosophy would be by reading Isaiah Berlin's essay 'Two Concepts of Liberty', in his *Four Essays on Liberty*. Other important modern contributions are J. Rawls, *A Theory of Justice* and R. Nozick, *Anarchy, State and Utopia*. It would be rewarding also to read two contributions from different political perspectives written earlier in the twentieth century, A. Gramsci's *Prison Notebooks* and F. A. Hayek's *The Road to Serfdom*.

For general discussion of several of the issues touched on in this chapter, see P. Singer, *Practical Ethics*; S. Hampshire (ed.), *Public and Private Morality*; R. Dworkin, *Taking Rights Seriously*; H. L. A. Hart, *Law, Liberty and Morality*. Specifically on the issue of human rights, see J. Waldron (ed.), *Theories of Rights*. On the ethical questions relating to war, see M. Walzer, *Just and Unjust Wars*, and R. Philips, *War and Justice*. For a selection of readings on these subjects, see R. Wasserstrom, *Today's Moral Problems*, or J. Rachels, *Moral Problems*. There is also a useful selection of recent articles in A. Quinton (ed.), *Political Philosophy*. Interesting recent general books relating to political philosophy are: J. Pelczynski and J. Gray (eds.), *Conceptions of Liberty in Political Philosophy* (essays on historical political philosophers seen in the light of Berlin's 'Two Concepts of Liberty'); A. Arblaster, *The Rise and Decline of Western Liberalism*; and John Gray, *Liberalism. Political Thought from Plato to Nato*, ed. B. Redhead, contains an excellent and authoritative set of essays on the main political philosophers of the Western tradition.

Classical sources

Plato: Dialogues, particularly *Republic*, *Laws*
Aristotle: *Politics*
Hobbes: *Leviathan*
Locke: *Two Treatises of Government*
Rousseau: *The Social Contract* and *Discourse on the Origins of Inequality*
J. S. Mill: *On Liberty*; *Representative Government*
K. Marx: *The Communist Manifesto*; or see D. McLellan (ed.), *Karl Marx: Selected Writings*.

4 Thinking about Reasoning

Can we isolate reason, and is it, so regarded, an
independent source of concepts and judgements which
spring from it alone?

— Immanuel Kant, *Critique of Pure Reason*

My existence as a thinking, deciding agent, then, and my ability to play a role as a moral or political influence or force, depend upon the accuracy of my beliefs. It is a commonplace that I cannot believe everything that I hear or that I read in the press, nor even that I apparently see on television. Most of what I see or hear in this way is illusion – I pay for fiction and make-believe. Can I trust those who tell me: 'This which you are seeing now is true'? Or: 'What I am giving you now are the facts'?

For political decisions such as those I have just been considering, I depend particularly on politicians and political activists for my information. But here I *know* that distortion, exaggeration, the emphasis on what it is in a person's interest to emphasize are the very stuff and form of politics. To confirm the facts in either of these cases may be more than I can attempt, given that I am simply a person, tied to a particular location at a particular time. Also, whatever the 'facts' are, there are, in a sense, too many of them, so that the selection of facts can itself mislead. But some claims that I hear I am able to judge without practical observation: these are the ones that involve the sort of sleight of hand mentioned by Berlin. Some of these I can already recognize from experience. Words are sometimes used with double or shifting meanings, with equivocation on one side, and misunderstanding on the other. There is question-begging assertion, where what is to be proved is assumed even before the argument begins. There are hasty generalizations, false analogies, slanted arguments. Essential aspects of an issue are neglected, cases advanced with insufficient argument. The irrelevant, the inconsistent and indeed the contradictory may all feature. In general, these may all result in arguments which do not lead to the conclusion being asserted or which end in contradictory claims. So can I find some general principles to chart a course through these hazards? Are there rules for clear thinking and right reasoning? Are there ways of avoiding error, of recognizing distortion or deliberate falsification?

I know, of course, that this has been a preoccupation of philosophy from its beginning, and so I turn first of all to those beginnings, where I find that the map of reasoning has already been sketched out by others.

First thoughts about reasoning

From the time when the philosopher Heraclitus (who flourished around 504/500 BC) said, 'You cannot step twice into the same river; for fresh waters are ever flowing in upon you,' Greek philosophers were impressed with the idea that hard knowledge is possible only when the mind encounters something unchanging and not subject to flux, to coming into existence and passing out of existence. This effectively rules out the world that the eye and ear encounter, since this is characterized by its impermanence and kaleidoscopic change. What remain, though, are certain formal structures to be considered as possible objects of knowledge. In particular, the worlds of numbers, of geometrical shapes and theorems and of logical relationships seem to have a constancy and reliability which make it possible to build up a firm body of knowledge where these are concerned. If there is truth to be arrived at in these matters, then it is, in a sense, unchanging truth. By contrast, if there is truth to be grasped in matters of fact – that a particular tree is in leaf, for example – this is a fleeting and ephemeral truth: it was not true previously, and there will certainly be another later time when it is not true. So whether my claim is true or not depends on where and when I make that claim.

But there seem to be other truths – those of geometry, for example – which are not restricted in this way. They seem to have an inbuilt formal or structural guarantee. These truths are necessary, where truths about matters of fact are merely contingent. Hence the appeal of *form*. (And Plato envisaged, whether metaphorically or otherwise, a world of timeless Forms – pure, abstract concepts and relationships like, for example, beauty or equality – known independently of ordinary human experience – independently, that is, of what can be observed by the senses.[1]) So, setting aside what might be established by observation, the Greeks gave priority to what might be called *structural* truth and falsity. And certain striking and paradoxical cases of falsity seemed to provide a particularly fascinating starting point. If following out the consequences of a statement could lead to contradictory conclusions, this was taken as showing that something must be wrong with it as a claim, although *what* was wrong was not necessarily equally clear. This illustrates the general point that it may be easier to see that something is wrong than to provide a satisfactory intellectual explanation as to why it is.

A good example of this is provided by what is probably the first known 'paradox'. The Cretan, Epimenides, was said to have uttered the statement:

'All Cretans are liars.'

Now if what he said was true, given that he was a Cretan, it follows that he was lying. If he wasn't, then, of course, he was demonstrating the falsity of his own assertion by showing that Cretans could, after all, be truthful. In other words, when Epimenides said, 'All Cretans are liars,' this statement was, if true, false; if false, true.

The paradox does not depend, though, on being uttered by a Cretan of ancient times. The same puzzle arises from considering, for instance:

'The sentence you are reading now is false'

or simply:

'I am lying.'

Probably the most famous paradoxes of ancient times, though, were those devised by Zeno of Elea (born *c*. 490 BC.) – paradoxes designed to shake people's complacency about their understanding of space, time, movement and mathematics. The best known of these is the paradox of Achilles and the tortoise. It consists in arguing:

> In a race between the fastest runner, Achilles, and a tortoise, if the tortoise is given a start on Achilles, Achilles will never catch it up. This is because, before he can get to the place where the tortoise is, Achilles must first get to the place where the tortoise *was*. But by the time he gets *there*, the tortoise will have moved on at least a little. There is no (logical) end to this stipulation (even though in practice it doesn't seem to affect the outcome!) So Achilles can never catch the tortoise.[2]

This paradox, unlike that of Epimenides, does not produce two contradictory conclusions, but instead just one conclusion which contradicts experience; in other words, it does not square with what actually happens. But what the two cases have in common is that a perfectly convincing-looking argument leads to an unacceptable conclusion.

Trying to see what is objectionable about such paradoxes suggests that I assume, perhaps unconsciously, certain very basic rules of thought. If I am obliged to draw as conclusions both 'I am lying' and also 'I am not lying', I am in effect being forced to assert both A and not-A – to break, that is, the law of non-contradiction. And the implication that both may be true violates another similar law: the law of the excluded middle, which says: Either A or not-A. Attempting to entertain such contradictory ideas jars in a way which is immediately or intuitively repugnant.

Greek thinkers looked for principles for drawing conclusions that would avoid both paradoxes and error, and the ways in which they tried to formalize the structure of argument lasted, I know, largely unchallenged through medieval times right up to the late nineteenth century and the beginning of the twentieth.

Reflecting on this, I ask myself whether I should not find out about contemporary moves in these fields of logic and reasoning. As it happens, I am not without the possibility of an informant.

Interlude: the story of Sophia

Many years ago I heard the story of Sophia. Sophia was born in 1900, the daughter of a wealthy and loving family. Owing to a physical infirmity, the nature of which I have not been able to discover, she has never left the comfortable book-lined study-bed-room in an ancient castle in Southern Ireland provided for her by her devoted parents, now long dead.

In her early years her great interest was the work of Bertrand Russell (1872–1970) – because of a precocious interest in mathematics, she had been given one of the first copies of Russell and Whitehead's *Principia Mathematica* – and she was fascinated by Wittgenstein's *Tractatus*, the importance of which she immediately recognized. In her thirties, it was Ayer's *Language, Truth and Logic* that stirred her interest and led her to consider ideas developed in Europe and the United States.

The two World Wars scarcely impinged on her life, but she was troubled and saddened by what she read at second hand of man's inhumanity to man. Her own situation made it impossible for her to play any part in the political, cultural or social life of her times, and she made no attempt to contact any of the figures and personalities whose work provided the interest and focus of her life.

Now in her eighties, she has shown herself willing to communicate with the younger members of her extensive family. A direct question on the subjects that interest her will always receive a direct answer, although I have noticed that, with failing eyesight and limited time left to her, Sophia never allows herself any of the usual social interchange of ordinary correspondence. But she knows and approves of my quest, and from time to time I shall write to her and record her replies.

This is the first letter I received from her on the subject of reasoning and argument:

First letter from Sophia

Dear Q,

I received your letter about logic, but I am afraid I am not able to help in any detailed way, since you are asking about an enterprise of enormous proportions. But I can tell you a little about the way the subject has been approached of late, and it will be for you to pursue in other ways to the limits of your own interests and capacities.

So let me begin by saying that arguments are not always clearly presented. They may be embedded in complex verbiage; made inconspicuous by irrelevant additions; obscured by redundant considerations; distorted by rhetorical flourishes; tied confusingly to other arguments; stretched, compressed, hinted at, or lost in unnecessary detail. Premisses may be suppressed; conclusions left unstated. Logic attempts to bring some kind of order into this jungle of possibilities by isolating the skeleton or bones of arguments. If you can acquire the habit of looking for this underlying structure, then perhaps you will be less susceptible to these various forms of either deliberate or unconscious obfuscation.

Typically, then, in an argument, evidence, reason or grounds in the form of **premisses** are presented as leading to a **conclusion**. So the structure of every argument can be represented like this:

<u>premiss(es)</u>
Therefore: conclusion

In practice, people may invert this order, or even not bother to mention every part of their argument explicitly. The essential point, though, is that inference does consist in drawing conclusions from premisses.

You will have noticed that arguments are sometimes described as sound, sometimes as correct, sometimes as valid, and that these terms are often used interchangeably in ordinary conversation. In the context of formal logic, though, it is necessary to be more precise. You may say of some arguments, for example, that they establish the truth of their conclusions. But it is possible to look at the formal structure or shape of an argument quite apart from the question on truth or falsity. What purely formal rules can supply is standards of logical correctness or validity. A correct or valid argument justifies its conclusion, but to know whether it establishes it or not, it would be necessary to know independently that the premisses are actually true.

For example, the conclusion 'white elephants fly' follows from 'all elephants fly'. That is, the argument is formally correct or valid. But, of course, the starting premiss is false. So it would be a mistake to assume that the conclusion has been proved, or established as true. Assessing the truth of the premiss of an argument is a different kind of undertaking from deciding whether the inference – from premiss to conclusion – is correct. To check whether all elephants fly, it would be necessary to do a little – though not very much! – factual investigation. But the inference is perfectly sound, and to check that, it is necessary to know something about correct and incorrect ways of arguing. The problem with the arguments of Epimenides and Zeno that you mentioned is that they look perfectly correct; it is hard to see what, if anything, is wrong with their premisses, and yet the conclusions, in both cases, suggest that they cannot be sound.

The contribution of logic is to suggest that there might – tricky cases like these apart – be patterns of argument which are always sound. That is to say, in these cases, if the premisses are true, then necessarily the conclusion is true as well. And equally reliably, an argument from true premisses to a false conclusion must be unsound. At the same time, there are other patterns of argument where, even if the premisses are true, this does not guarantee the truth of the conclusion. Establishing the truth of the premisses, though, is in either case a completely different kind of enterprise. The Stoic logicians provided a compelling metaphor of the different degrees of assent one might give to the kind of factual assertion that often features as the premiss of an argument. Their comparison was with a more or less tightly clenched hand or fist. Simply imagining something – like a flying elephant – would be like the hand spread out. But there is a spectrum of degrees of assent from there, through belief and understanding to the clear or firm knowledge that would be metaphorically represented by the firm grasp of hand surrounding fist. In the end, the Stoics came to think that we might aspire only to probability on matters of fact, but the essential claim they made was that, as far as reasoning was concerned, there were some argument 'shapes' that did give certainty.

Two main kinds of argument-form were identified in classical times: those which take the form of syllogisms and were extensively categorized by Aristotle;[3] and those which centre on the 'if . . . then' relationship, and which were systematized by the Stoics.[4]

Aristotelian logic operates on statements which are, in a grammatical sense, of subject–predicate form: in particular Aristotle explored the relations between four kinds of statement: affirmative assertions, such as 'All fat people are greedy' and 'Some diseases are curable'; and negative assertions, such as 'No cats are purple' and 'Some dogs are not trainable'. A typical argument constructed from these sorts of building-blocks would be:

> All politicians are controversial figures
> All controversial figures are the subject of media interest

---

Therefore: All politicians are the subject of media interest

Since an indefinite number of arguments have the same form, irrespective even of what language they are expressed in, being able to pick out the form provides a means for checking their validity. And not all arguments of this type – called a syllogism – are valid. For example, it is not correct to reason:

> No royal persons are controversial figures
> Some controversial figures are seen on television

Therefore: No royal persons are seen on television

Why is this wrong? Well, even if we accept that some controversial figures are seen on television, this is perfectly consistent with some other people – who could, after all, be royals – appearing on television as well. In other words, none of our assumptions preclude royals appearing on television – as, of course, they do!

There are many possible varieties of arguments like these, and many possible categorical syllogisms, some valid, some invalid. But certain problems were implicit even within the structure of valid syllogisms. For example, in Aristotelian logic, it was assumed that the subject of an 'all As are Bs' statement did exist. But it is sometimes necessary to make statements of this form – which can be true statements – without assuming existence. That is so in the case of the First Law of Motion – a perfectly useful and true statement that does not involve an assumption of existence: 'All objects free from impressed forces persevere in a state of rest or in uniform motion in a straight line.'

To retain the possibility of making uncommitted statements like this, modern logic has abandoned the assumption that if 'all As are Bs', then there do exist some As which are Bs. So, for example, to say 'All dogs are carnivorous' is not to say that there are dogs. Instead, the assertion is to be understood as:

> 'For any x, if that x is a dog, then that x is carnivorous.'

For the inference to 'Some dogs are carnivorous' to follow, it would be necessary to add explicitly, as an extra premiss, that 'dogs exist'. But this produces a gap between logic and ordinary language – a consequence which many modern logicians have preferred to accept. Ordinary language is in fact closer to traditional than to modern logic in its implications, for in ordinary language, if someone says, 'All my investments are prospering,' it would seem odd to discover that he or she has no investments. On the other hand, 'All truly good people are free from envy' does not carry the message that there are any such people, so there clearly are ordinary language uses corresponding to the interpretation of 'All' in modern logic, even if these are comparatively rare.

This will give you some idea of the state of the subject when I first became interested in it – I was, of course, only a child then, but topics like these have always fascinated me. I will write to you again about more recent developments.

Yours,
Sophia

I had scarcely had time to reflect on Sophia's account of traditional logic when her second letter arrived.

Second letter from Sophia

Dear Q,

I said that I would write to you about modern logic. This is usually taken as beginning with the work of the mathematician and logician Gottlob Frege (1848–1925), and it was further developed by Bertrand Russell (1872–1970). There is a developed system of predicate logic which introduces the clarity and power of symbols into some of the areas I mentioned in my previous letter. However, unlike Aristotle, who was mainly concerned with structure within sentences, modern logicians, like the ancient Stoics, have also given a good deal of time and attention to reasoning which takes whole sentences or propositions as the units for its operations.

This has been done by developing the notion of a logical system. I can best explain this by giving you an outline of a simple one. Its components are:

(a) letters used to represent simple, affirmative sentences: usually p, q, r, s, etc., but sometimes p, p′, p″, p‴, etc. (If one thinks of programming a computer to do logic, or if, for more complex logical reasoning, an infinite stock of letters is required, then the advantage of the latter system is apparent. But the human mind is probably better able to cope with the former.)

(b) brackets to act as the punctuation marks of complex sentences by indicating the scope of a sign. For example, 'p or q and r' is ambiguous: but brackets can differentiate '(p or q) and r' from 'p or (q and r)'. This is parallel to the way that in algebra '3+5×2' is ambiguous, but can be made unambiguous by brackets indicating either '(3+5)×2' or '3+(5×2)'.

(c) symbols for logical constants: these are terms which provide the structure or form of an argument. The constants which are used vary in different systems; since some can be reduced to others, it is in fact possible to work with only two, for

example negation and disjunction. There are, then, different conventions. But a commonly used set of constants would be: 'and' (conjunction), 'or' (disjunction), 'not' (negation), 'if . . . then' (the conditional) and 'if and only if' (the bi-conditional), sometimes written 'iff'. To signify these, special symbols are used. One in common use represents these logical constants as respectively:

conjunction	·
disjunction	v
negation	~
conditional	⊃
bi-conditional	≡

Although these correspond quite closely to the relationships indicated by the English language expressions used to explain them, the main reason for introducing them is that they can be made more specific and less ambiguous than ordinary language. There are, though, some important differences. The two most striking divergences are these:

(i) 'or', as indicated by the sign 'v' in 'p v q', is not exclusive: it is true if both alternatives are true, as well as if only one of them is. So in this notation 'Either he is innocent or he is a very good actor' does not mean, as it probably would in ordinary conversation, that he must be one or the other – he could be both.

and (ii) the conditional expressed by the hook '⊃' has an entirely distinctive meaning: this is that 'p⊃q' is false only when 'p' is true and 'q' false. In ordinary life, 'If you sue me then I will become bankrupt' may be taken to imply a causal relationship, or at least some kind of dependence between the two parts of the compound sentence. But this is not the case where the conditional expressed by the hook is concerned. The causal aspect is omitted, leaving only the bare logical relationship.

This kind of conditional is not, however, an invention of modern logic. In fact, it was first recognized by the Stoic logicians, whose interests centred on the different ways that 'if . . . then' can be used to form valid and invalid arguments. A classic example of this is the argument known as Modus Ponens. For example:

> If he has sued her, she is bankrupt
> He has sued her
> _____
> So she is bankrupt

In the symbolism of modern logic, this becomes:

$$p \supset q$$
$$p$$
$$\therefore q$$

The form displayed by these symbols is a valid form. That is, every argument which takes this form is valid. So this is a valid argument.

By contrast, if someone else were to reason:

> If he has sued her, then she is bankrupt
> She is bankrupt
> _____
> So he has sued her

then the reasoning can be symbolically presented as

$$p \supset q$$
$$q$$
$$\therefore p$$

and this is an invalid form. The argument is indeed invalid, as one might see by reflecting that there are many other ways to become bankrupt. The appeal to this invalid form is a common error of reasoning – that is, a fallacy. Indeed, it is so common that it has a name; it is known as the Fallacy of Affirming the Consequent. (In an 'if . . . then' statement, the statement following 'if' is known as the antecedent; the statement following 'then' is known as the consequent.) This invalid statement is not to be confused with another valid form of argument called Modus Tollens:

> If he has sued her, she is bankrupt
> She is not bankrupt
> _____
> So he has not sued her

or

$$p \supset q$$
$$\sim q$$
$$\therefore \ \sim p$$

There are, of course, many other valid forms of argument, and many other invalid ones. The conditional that is involved is recognizable as corresponding to some extent to the way in which 'if . . . then' is used in ordinary language. All the same, it is accepted as having two consequences which are so surprising, and so divorced from ordinary language, that they have been described as 'paradoxes' of material implication.

What these 'paradoxes' amount to is that, because of the meaning given to the sign '$\supset$', a false statement implies any statement whatsoever. Also, any true statement is implied by any statement whatsoever. This is because the only way in which '$p \supset q$' can be falsified is by finding a situation in which 'p' is true and 'q' false. This can never happen (a) if 'p' is false nor (b) if 'q' is true. Hence the so-called 'paradoxes'.

This results in other mismatches between logic and ordinary reasoning. For example, if in the above example 'p' is a contradiction or an absurdity, then it cannot be true. Therefore, anything at all follows from a contradiction or an absurdity.

If some of these relationships appear surprising, they can be checked by a useful mechanical method, which consists in setting out truth tables which make it possible to read off the implications of various assumptions. The simplest truth table, with T standing for 'true' and F for 'false', could be set out like this:

p
—
T
F

Whatever 'p' and '$\sim p$' stand for, they cannot both be true. So two possible combinations of a proposition and its denial can be set out in a truth table:

	p	~p
1.	T	F
2.	F	T

The complex assertion 'p.q' (p and q) generates a more complicated truth table:

p	q	p.q
T	T	T
T	F	F
F	T	F
F	F	F

(This truth table is built up by first filling in the possibilities under p and under q, and then filling in the final column.)

The conditional can be expressed most clearly with a truth table:

p	q	p⊃q
T	T	T
T	F	F
F	T	T
F	F	T

Obviously, the more complicated arguments become, the longer and more complicated become the truth tables.

The paradoxes of material implication and the system of truth tables taken together display both the defects and the merits of logical systems. On the merit side, it is an advantage of formal systems that they do provide mechanical means, such as truth tables, for testing for truth. The letters 'p', 'q', 'r', etc., are used as place-markers or tokens which can stand in for many different sentences, and the truth of a complex sentence is entirely a matter *of the truth and falsity of its component sentences. This characteristic, known as truth-functionality, is a central advantage of formalizing arguments.*

But there are also disadvantages, and these raise such new considerations that I shall write to you again about them in a little while.

> Yours,
> Sophia

And indeed, within a very short time, the following letter reached me.

Third letter from Sophia

Dear Q,

As I said in my last letter to you, a logical language is more precise and more rigorous than a natural language. But this advantage brings some corresponding disadvantages. In particular the gap between logic and ordinary language presents a problem.

Certain kinds of assertions, for instance, do not fit into the pattern just described. These are, in particular, assertions about psychological states such as beliefs, desires or wishes. The use of verbs like 'believe' or 'want' is a sign of contexts which are called 'intensional'. The terms 'intensional' and its opposite 'extensional' refer to the possibility of substitution without change of truth. You may be able to see what I mean from this example: if Humphrey Bogart is the film star who played opposite Bergman in Casablanca, then it seems I ought to be able to substitute the description 'the film star who played opposite Bergman in Casablanca' in any statement containing 'Humphrey Bogart' as a term, without changing the truth or falsity of the statement. I can do this, for example, in the brief statement: 'If Humphrey Bogart was a successful actor he must have been rich.' 'Humphrey Bogart', then, is used extensionally in this context.

But there are contexts in which this kind of substitution will not work. For example, suppose I truthfully say:

> 'I believe that Humphrey Bogart never played opposite Bergman.'

Now the fact is that Humphrey Bogart did play opposite Bergman in Casablanca. But I certainly could not substitute for 'Humphrey Bogart' the phrase 'the actor who played opposite Bergman in Casablanca' since this would turn my statement into:

> 'I believe that the actor who played opposite Bergman in Casablanca never played opposite Bergman'

– something I definitely do not believe. Or suppose someone says:

> 'I wish that I had met Bogart.'

Again, if the speaker believes Bogart never played opposite Bergman it would not be correct to assume he was asserting

> 'I wish that I had met the actor who played opposite Bergman in Casablanca.'

It seems then that a different type of logic is needed for evaluating reasoning in intensional contexts like this. Something else is needed, too, to account for certain other important non-truth-functional contexts – those that involve reference to necessity and possibility. For to say something is necessary or possible is not the same as to say that it is true or false.

Modal logic deals specifically with the problem of talking about necessity and possibility. In addition, intuitionist and relevant logics have been devised, which are based on abandoning those consequences of propositional or predicate logic which do not fit with the reasoning people intuitively take to be sound, or which are irrelevant to the kind of arguments they sometimes wish to conduct in the more flexible style of ordinary life. (So, for example, these logics may abandon the tenet that anything follows from a contradiction.) The intention is to preserve the rigour of a logical system without offending against the logical intuitions most people would claim. It is true that all valid forms of argument prevent a move from the true to the false. They keep the careful reasoner on the path of truth, once that path has been entered. But some of these valid arguments suffer from irrelevance, redundancy, or circularity. So there is some reason for thinking we should be more selective in our acceptance of 'valid' argument forms. So-called relevant logics attempt to do just that.

A central problem concerns 'if . . . then'. How is it possible to draw significant conclusions from unfulfilled conditionals? For example, people are prepared to debate seriously the rival claims of:

> 1. 'If Churchill were Prime Minister now, Britain and America would have closer ties.'

and

> 2. 'If Churchill were Prime Minister now, Britain and America would be further apart.'

Propositional logic, however, cannot take account of this kind of contrast. One recent method proposed for dealing with the troublesome conditionals is to turn them into more tractable and amenable categorical ones. This is achieved by the introduction of a language of possible worlds.

This is not entirely a new notion. The philosopher Gottfried Wilhelm Leibniz (1646–1716) envisaged an infinity of possible worlds conceived as ideas in God's mind, and he suggested that something was necessarily true if it was true in all possible worlds. He claimed that the actual world we live in is selected by God from the infinity of possibilities. Leibniz's interest in proposing this theory was primarily logical and metaphysical, but it was interpreted by the French writer Voltaire (1694–1778) as expressing a naïve religiously-based optimism. Voltaire's novel, Candide, is a saga of human woes and misfortunes featuring a philosopher, Dr Pangloss, whose doctrine consists simply in the belief that this is the best of all possible worlds – a belief which Voltaire cynically, but convincingly, throws into question.[5]

The idea of things or items which are not actual has been employed more recently by Alexius Meinong (1853–1920), who believed it necessary to accept that true and false statements could be made about items – for example, round squares or golden mountains – which do not exist. Otherwise, he argued, there is a problem in explaining what we talk about when we refer to non-existent entities. Even if we say 'golden mountains do not exist' or 'round squares cannot even be imagined', it seems that there must be something, in some sense, to which we refer, even if we only go on and deny its existence or its imaginability. So, it could be said, in some quite literal sense there really are these possibilities; and even, there really are these impossibilities.[6]

The contemporary debate is again conducted in terms of possible worlds: this time possible worlds are the names of states of affairs – possibilities or structures which might obtain; while actual worlds are realized states of affairs – actualized possibilities or structures which the world does contain. Thus possibility and necessity are represented like this:

> Something is necessarily true if it is true in all possible worlds.

> Something is possibly true if it is true in a possible world.

> Something is necessarily not true if there is no possible world in which it is true.

> Something is possibly not true if there is a possible world in which it is not true.

The contemporary American philosopher David Lewis (b. 1941), who is an exponent of a theory of possible worlds, believes that what makes this world the actual one is simply that this is the world we are in. In his view, there are infinitely many other worlds with other people in them which are actual for those people. Lewis's position is known as modal realism.[7] It is a position which seems a long way from common sense, but if it were to be rejected for this reason alone, then it would be equally necessary to reject most of modern physics for the same reason.

The advantage of this type of theory is that it explains statements like 'Possibly there is a primeval creature in Loch Ness' or, 'Possibly there is life on Venus', turning them into the kind of statements that can be more easily handled by logic. It has the further advantage that it makes it possible to reason about unfulfilled conditionals – something that may, after all, be quite important. Take, for instance, 'If there were a world government,

the people of the world would live in peace.' Conventional ways
of dealing with the notion of possibility reduce it to consistency,
but a great many assertions are consistent (that is, not logically
contradictory) which are nevertheless impossible. For example,
there is no inconsistency in supposing that David Lewis might
have known Leibniz and discussed the matter of possible worlds
with him; but it is nevertheless impossible!

I will leave you to think about these things and to pursue the
study of formal logic, if it appeals to you, in other ways and with
other teachers. Meanwhile there is one other important area of
reasoning that I must write to you about if we are to complete our
inquiries on these matters.

> Yours,
> Sophia

Sophia was as good as her word, and soon afterwards I received this
final letter from her on the subject of reasoning:

Fourth letter from Sophia

Dear Q,

As I indicated in my last letter, logic may be able, in one way or
another, to handle reasoning concerned with the merely possible.
And so it may also be able to deal with 'if . . . then' sentences in
which some stronger relation is asserted between p and q. Clearly,
something more than a purely formal relationship is needed for
science, which deals in probabilities, rather than in the straight
deduction which is the hallmark of logical systems.

Another type of argument seems to be involved here, although
its formal structure may look fairly similar. In ordinary life, it is
much more common to find arguments such as the one implied in
the following conversation:

> First Speaker: Matt is a farmer, so I expect he is a
> conservative.
> Second speaker: Why do you suppose that?
> First speaker: Because most farmers are conservatives –
> ninety per cent according to the latest opinion poll.

Formally set out, this argument might be presented like this:

> 90% of farmers are conservatives
> Matt is a farmer
> _____

Therefore: probably Matt is a conservative.

or, more briefly:

> p
> _____

Therefore: probably q

In spite of the similarity of form, arguments like these do differ in important ways from the deductive ones so far considered. In particular, if I argue deductively:

> All logicians are pedantic
> Susan is a logician
> _____

my conclusion will not be in any way undermined if I add to my premisses. For example:

> All logicians are pedantic
> Susan is a logician and she is a mother

In a deductive argument, 'Susan is pedantic' does follow. But if you add to the premisses in the present case, the result can be strikingly affected. For example:

> Ninety per cent of farmers are conservatives
> Matt is a farmer and he is founder of the Farmers'
> Revolutionary Front

In this case, 'Probably Matt is a conservative' does not follow. It is highly unlikely that he is!

   These pitfalls are more evident in the case of the inferences of Agatha Christie's sleuths, Poirot or Miss Marple; or in the assumptions behind opinion polls which take a limited sample of people and then go on to make predictions about who will win the next election.

Agatha Christie's sleuths are often engaged in reasoning within the compass of psychology – their deductions concern the motivation and actions of indvidual people. The opinion pollsters are concerned with the social sciences in a more general way – sociology, demography, social psychology all play a part here. But since people are more complex than things (and, what is more, the investigators are themselves part of what is being investigated), it may be easier to see what is involved in these kinds of reasoning by analogy with what goes on in the 'harder' areas of the physical sciences.

Scientific method has, in the past, been seen as a part of the science of logic. But in order to make it fit the pattern of logical – that is to say, deductive – reasoning, it is necessary to add an extra premiss to the type of argument which seems to typify scientific reasoning. It seems that a premiss of a universal nature is needed to unite particular observations. For example, it is possible to infer that your own particular cat – I think she is called Otteline, isn't she? – is a nocturnal creature, if you know that all cats are nocturnal.

On the whole, it is tempting to think that science works by discovering such general laws – not always quite as obvious as that one, of course! – and it can hardly be denied that the assumption that there are such laws has been fruitful. But these laws unfortunately have to assume what they set out to prove – i.e. the reference to 'all cats' is already a reference to Otteline. So either the particular or the universal claim is a reference to what must be strictly unknowable. The British philosopher David Hume (1711–76) put the problem in this way: 'It is impossible to guarantee, that an unknown instance of the property A will also exhibit the property B, if A and B are different properties.'[8]

Kant resisted the scepticism implied by Hume, arguing that the truth of causal laws has to be taken as a presupposition of human thought.[9] And it does seem to be necessary to make some assumptions about the future which (a) are not necessarily true and (b) can in any case be no better than claims. Science itself does not suppose that the world will continue for ever as it is now, and yet it seems that the assumption involved in scientific reasoning – called induction – is precisely this – that the future will resemble the past.

Bertrand Russell once suggested that this assumption is rather like that of a chicken in the farmyard, which has come to expect to have a handful of corn thrown to it each morning, is continually reinforced in this belief, but ultimately finds that one morning the farmer has come out to wring its neck.[10]

Nevertheless, science has shown itself of considerably more use to human beings than the chicken's hypothesis is to the chicken. This is why the term 'scientific' functions as a prestige-word when applied to reasoning. Science is the name given to any inquiry which takes as its object describing, explaining and predicting occurrences in the natural world. It is distinguished from unscientific attempts to do these things by the fact that it looks for warranted or justified claims on which to base its conclusions. In particular, for an inquiry to be scientific it is necessary that it accept, as a standard, testing by empirical means. (An empirical test is a test carried out in terms of observation by the senses.) The form that scientific inquiry takes, then, is this:

Problem → hypothesis → drawing conclusions from the hypothesis → testing the conclusions against experience → interpreting the results.

In the past, the final stage of a sequence like this would be described as confirmation or refutation. It was thought, that is, that scientific theories could be rigorously derived from experience, by observation and experiment – a view popular since Sir Francis Bacon (1561–1626), Galileo (1564–1642) and Sir Isaac Newton (1642–1727) replaced the view, prevalent from Aristotle to medieval times, that it was possible to sit down and work out from first principles how things – like the movement of the planets – ought to be, with the more fruitful idea of seeking by observation to determine how things are. This is, of course, the method of experiment. But unless it is possible to solve the problem of induction by showing how the assumption that the future will resemble the past is justified, it seems that confirmation is out of the question.

Some people, though, would say that confirmation is not necessary. It may be equally useful for practical purposes to be able to show conclusively that some hypotheses are wrong, even if it is impossible to show that any are right. This solution to the problem of induction has been proposed by Karl Popper (b. 1902). According to Popper, human knowledge is a matter of conjectures and refutations rather than of established certainty, and scientific 'laws' survive, rather like species in Darwin's theory of evolution, only until they have been effectively refuted by some inconsistent finding.[11]

As far as probabilities are concerned, though, Popper's view is firmer and more 'objectivist' than that of subsequent critics. The probability of a die falling in a particular way, for instance, is in his view a matter of an objective propensity of the die. Others, however, have insisted on interpreting the probability of a die falling in a certain way subjectively: that is, as a matter of our willingness to bet on it falling that way. This kind of computation has been developed to a high degree of mathematical sophistication, with analogies from games and gambling, but its effect is to make of science a closed rather than an open system. Pursuing the gambling analogy, in any race there are a finite number of horses. But science, as it is usually conceived, is open to considering indefinitely many different hypotheses. But if Popper seems to have challenged the credentials of science as something resting on a firm inferential base – if he has shown that there cannot be such a thing as inductive logic – he still believes in a logic of inquiry. That is to say, he does not want to explain away the procedures of scientific inference by explaining scientific discovery in terms of the psychology of scientists, nor does he suggest that our ways of construing the world change by some inevitable historical process.

Subsequent reflection on the philosophy of science has been less optimistic and more relativistic in its approach. You will probably accept that it may be a mistake to think that any method exists by which scientific theories can be 'proved true'; perhaps you will doubt whether they can even be conclusively proved false. But, all the same, it seems there is a concept of scientific method which serves to separate science from pseudo-science.

Some theories are more deserving of attention than others. Few scientists would take seriously, for example, astrology, numerology or flat-earthism. But all the same, some distinctly unscientific beliefs, no better grounded than these, can be very fiercely held – as are these, of course, by their supporters. It is not so unusual to find people rejecting Darwin's theory of evolution in spite of fossil and geological evidence because they want, for other reasons, to believe that the earth, together with human and animal life, was created in 4004 BC. These pseudo-scientists are no doubt best recognized by the fact that they refuse to accept the burden of proof.

Even if you dismiss these, though, along with the occult and the obscurantist, you may still wonder how to justify the day-to-day scientific and practical assumptions of ordinary life. Rather than concede that any belief or claim is as good as any other, you might prefer to scale down your claim and simply say that confirmation is increased, the more instances you are able to gather, of some belief of yours being true. For example, the claim at issue might be about the tendency of metals to expand when heated. It seems plausible to argue that the more instances you can assemble, the greater the probability of the universal claim. The problem is, though, that no matter how many observations you make, they are going to be finite in number, while the claim that is made by a scientific generalization like 'All metals expand when heated' is potentially infinite in scope.

This could be called the problem of the necessarily inadequate number of cases . . . But if you take another example, it might seem that scientific probability is not a matter of piling up instances at all. To test 'Acid turns litmus paper red' it would be normal to experiment on only a limited number of occasions – the later ones only for demonstration purposes, or as a check, perhaps, that nothing had gone wrong the first time. The important thing is the background of theory to the experiment. Or, as Hume remarked, a single experience of being burned by fire is normally sufficient to convince someone that fire burns.

Should the attempt at justification be abandoned, then, in the face of these difficulties? Could it, perhaps, be the case that science is not a rational activity at all? Philosophers of science

like Paul Feyerabend (b. 1924) are prepared to make this claim.
According to Feyerabend, science, although it seems to have
become our modern religion, has no better claim on our support
than Voodoo.[12] Whatever method is proposed in scientific inquiry,
Feyerabend argues, there will always be circumstances in which
that method is not the best one to follow. In other words, it will be
necessary to violate any rule at some time in order to make
scientific progress.

A reply which avoids this degree of scepticism, whilst at the
same time challenging many naïve assumptions, is offered by
Thomas Kuhn, in The Structure of Scientific Revolutions. The
central idea here is that of paradigms – theories accepted as
'normal science' at any one time.[13] In this book, Kuhn argues that
the history of science is not a mere cumulative account of
scientific knowledge, wrong theories being mere myths; on the
contrary, wrong theories were as valid for their practitioners at the
time as contemporary scientific theories are for us. Scientific
revolutions are, Kuhn argues, the displacement of one perspective
or paradigm by a new one. The 'discoveries' of science are simply
fruitful research programmes.

Theories which displace others to become the new paradigms
are defined by two characteristics:

  1. They must be revolutionary enough to attract an
enduring group away from received views, and

  2. They must be open-ended enough to leave problems
for the new group to resolve.

Scientific work, then, within such a paradigm, consists of: (a)
determining which facts are significant, (b) matching facts with
theory, and (c) articulating and defining the theory. Paradigms are
supplanted by new ones on the discovery of anomalies – instances
where the facts fail to fit the theory. But a single falsification, of
the kind emphasized by Popper, is not, Kuhn points out, sufficient
to cause scientists to reject an existing paradigm – they reject it
only when a new paradigm exists with which to compare both it
and nature. Falsification on its own would discredit the scientist
and not the theory.

Paradigm change within the sciences, according to Kuhn, is a
process like political revolution: it occurs through a challenge

from outside the accepted framework, and ultimately depends on either persuasion or force. The determining factor is simply the assent of the relevant community.

Instead of the traditional view in which sensory experience is conceived of as fixed and neutral, while theories are seen as man-made interpretations of given data, Kuhn suggests that what are called 'data' are in fact specially selected for attention because they fit in with the accepted paradigm.

Popper's shift to the notion of falsification rather than verification is seen by Kuhn as essentially within the traditional empiricist conception of science. For falsification of one theory is only confirmation of a competing one, and the fact is that science is selective in the data of which it takes account, whether there are confirming or falsifying instances. Paradigm-shift is something much more radical: it alters the parameters within which the problem is viewed.

You can probably accept, then, that even defining the problem is a matter of creative innovation where the goal of achieving scientific knowledge is concerned. Steam had pushed the lids off pots for many years before James Watt recognized it as an interesting phenomenon and went on to see steam as a source of power. Formulating a hypothesis, then, is itself dependent on context and on a certain kind of background knowledge.

Your answer, then, to the question about reasoning, that initially prompted my observations, must vary according to the type of reasoning that is in question. In particular, reasoning in practical affairs and in science employs different methods and standards from those involved in abstract or logical reasoning.

To see what this distinction amounts to, ask yourself: which of my beliefs would – or should – I continue holding even without any further justification? At first, having adopted a policy of taking everything as open to question, you may be inclined to answer, with some indignation, 'But none, of course.' However, as I have, I hope, persuaded you, some structures of reasoning do impose their own constraints. You do not, of course, have to be rational, but it is a condition of your rationality that you respect that distinctive phenomenon, logical truth. You may assert contradictions, and hear others assert them. But then you will have deserted the commitments with which you commenced your inquiry. So the answer 'None' will not do. But, then, neither, as you have seen, will the unqualified answer: 'Only beliefs which are directly based on observation.'

The question, though, is how widely logical truth can be construed, and whether, in fact, there is substantial truth to be found beyond the limits of sense-observation. Philosophers within the empiricist tradition have guarded the borderline between logical and empirical truth jealously, and have taken a frugal view of the applications of logical truth.

For empiricists, logical truth must either be explained as essentially empty – tautologous – or else, as J. S. Mill suggested, as a kind of empirical generalization.[14] In general terms, empiricism is the view that the senses are the only source of substantive human knowledge. It is the theory represented in particular by the British empiricist philosophers John Locke, George Berkeley (1685–1753) and David Hume. More recently, the tradition is represented by those philosophers, including particularly the logical positivists, who discuss the issue in terms of meaning and intelligibility, claiming simply that all bona fide ideas must be derived from experience.

Hume's famous formulation of the principle involved is couched in these terms:

> If we take in our hand any volume; of divinity or school metaphysics, for instance; let us ask, Does it contain any abstract reasoning concerning quantity or number? No. Does it contain any experimental reasoning concerning matter of fact and existence? No. Commit it then to the flames; for it can contain nothing but sophistry and illusion.[15]

The task for empiricism is essentially a matter of explaining, in terms of experience alone, all the knowledge we appear to have that cannot immediately be seen to derive from the senses: for example, knowledge of the self, of causation, of material objects, time, or other minds. The problem is that empiricism can very easily end up as scepticism (doubt that it is possible to know anything) or solipsism (the doctrine that all I can know about is states of myself). This problem is implicit in the tactic of basing knowledge on experience. For experience is a subjective, private phenomenon, from which it is difficult, if not impossible, to move to an objective world – a world that is public and open to different observers.

As the extract from Descartes' Meditations, which you mentioned in your letter to me, showed, the rationalist preference is, by contrast, for pure reason as the path to knowledge. It is based on the idea that it is possible to arrive at knowledge through pure thought.

Empiricist ideas in the twentieth century were pressed strongly by the philosophers of the Vienna Circle – a group which formed round the philosopher Moritz Schlick (1882–1936) in Vienna from 1922 on. The group, which was science- and logic-orientated, was united in its condemnation of metaphysics and its acceptance of the verification principle. This was the principle that, at a minimum, ruled out a statement as meaningless if no empirical observation could conceivably be relevant to determining whether it was true or false. It could loosely be formulated as: 'a statement is meaningful only if there is a way in which it could – at least in principle – be verified or tested'. At the same time analytic statements (including those of logic and mathematics) were interpreted as tautologies, and ethical judgements were analysed as not being statements at all, but expressions of emotion.

The ideas of the Vienna Circle were made widely known in Britain on the publication by A. J. Ayer of Language, Truth and Logic (1936), while the dispersal of members of the Vienna Circle to America and elsewhere as a result of the rise of Nazi power gave their ideas yet wider circulation and influence.[16]

These philosophical debates – and in particular the contrast between rationalism and empiricism – provide the backdrop for your present inquiry. But it is the preoccupation with empirical facts that is most relevant to your concerns. Clearly, for the sort of problems from which you started, it is empirical reasoning or judgement that you are most interested in. And it is judgement in particular that must concern you next, since empirical reasoning,

as I have indicated, must take as its premises empirical
judgements. I wish you well in your inquiry.
> Yours,
> Sophia

These, then, were the letters I received from my elderly informant
and they have, indeed, thrown some light on my inquiry. At the
outset, I took it that there were facts, and that these facts were important to my moral and political stance and to the way I construed the
world. Bad argument, I now see, can separate me from the facts, but
it seems that argument alone cannot establish what those facts are.
How, then, am I to arrive at knowledge? If I am to judge what other
people tell me, then my picture of what is the case is inevitably
going to be mediated by the language that they use. So, to place my
judgement in some relation to the facts, I must form some view of
the role of this intermediary – language – in interpreting events and
describing what is the case.

Notes to Chapter 4

1. For Plato's Theory of Forms, sometimes called the Theory of Ideas, see
   in particular the dialogues *Phaedo, Phaedrus, Republic* and *Meno*. The
   Greek word for Form is *eidos* (our *idea*), which can mean form in the
   sense of shape or outline. Here it means something more like nature or
   essence. The Theory of Forms was both a logical theory about universal
   terms, including mathematical concepts, and also a metaphysical
   doctrine about the independent and objective existence of important
   moral qualities.
2. Not everyone would agree that Zeno's arguments are sound. They may
   include, for instance, suppressed (i.e. tacit or unstated) premises which
   are false. The debate about Zeno, which continues to be a matter of
   interest and controversy to logicians and mathematicians, can be
   explored in a collection of articles by different authors, *Zeno's Para-*
   doxes, ed. Wesley C. Salmon.
   Such fragments as have survived of the works or sayings of early
   Greek (pre-Socratic) philosophers including Heraclitus, Parmenides and
   Zeno are gathered and readably explained in J. Burnet's *Early Greek*
   Philosophy. Parmenides resisted Heraclitus' doctrine of flux with a
   theory that denied the reality of change and motion. It was to defend
   Parmenides' position that Zeno propounded his paradoxes, designed to

show that the assumptions of Parmenides' opponents were just as much in conflict with observable fact as were those of Parmenides himself.

3. Aristotle's logical system was set out in his Organon, which comprises the Categories, On Interpretation, Prior and Posterior Analytics, Topics and On Sophistical Refutations.

4. For an account of Stoic logic, see John M. Rist (ed.), The Stoics, Ch. 1.

5. Voltaire, Candide, ou L'Optimisme. Voltaire's satirical talents were displayed in his portrayal of Dr Pangloss, whose ramblings parodied the views of Leibniz. Although he rejected the view that suffering and evil contribute to the good of the whole, Voltaire nevertheless believed it was worth working for the betterment of human conditions. While the famous remark at the end of Candide, 'Il faut cultiver notre jardin', could be taken as recommending a retreat from the world, it could also be regarded as recommending a return to the tasks closest to hand.
Leibniz Monadology is included in Leibniz: Philosophical Writings, trans. M. Morris.

6. There is considerable disagreement as to what Meinong claimed. There is currently, however, renewed interest in his ideas. See, for example, a recent defence of his position in an article by R. and V. Routley in Revue internationale de philosophie, 1973.

7. It is put forward in D. Lewis, On the Plurality of Worlds. 'Possible worlds' were mentioned by R. Carnap in his Meaning and Necessity in 1947, echoing Wittgenstein's reference to 'possible states of affairs' in the latter's Tractatus Logico-philosophicus.

8. Hume's views on induction and causal reasoning are set out in his Treatise of Human Nature, Book 1, Part 3. Kant said that Hume's radical scepticism woke him from his 'dogmatic slumbers' on this issue.

9. See I. Kant, Critique of Pure Reason, B 472–B 475. Kant sets out an antinomy concerning causality: on the one hand, it is possible to argue that 'causality in accordance with laws of nature is not the only causality'. On the other hand, however, there is a strong case for believing that 'everything in the world takes place solely in accordance with laws of nature'. This antinomy – two chains of reasoning leading to opposed conclusions – is resolved by applying the notion of the first type of causality to the world that is the object of our knowledge – a world which Kant sees as our construction – and leaving open the possibility that another type of causality applies to the world that lies behind the world of appearances, but which is beyond our knowledge.

10. B. Russell, The Problems of Philosophy, Ch. 6.

11. K. Popper, The Logic of Scientific Discovery. See also his Conjectures and Refutations and Objective Knowledge.

12. P. Feyerabend, Against method: a defence of anarchy.

13. T. Kuhn, The Structure of Scientific Revolutions. Some of the debate that followed publication of this book can be found in, for example, I. Lakatos and A. Musgrave (eds.), Criticism and the Growth of Knowledge, and

in I. Hacking (ed.), *Scientific Revolutions*. Kuhn is a physicist turned historian, whose influence on the philosophy of science has been considerable. His theory of paradigm change has been widely applied, particularly within the social sciences.

14. See J. S. Mill, *A System of Logic*, Book II, Ch. 4. In Book III, Chs. 8–10 of his classic study of eliminative induction, Mill went on to classify and categorize the methods of scientific investigation. The principles Mill set out for locating and identifying some causal factors and eliminating others form a useful guide to experimental inquiry.

15. D. Hume, *An Enquiry concerning Human Understanding* Sec. XII, Part III.

16. For a succinct account of logical positivism and the history of the Vienna Circle, see A. J. Ayer *et al. The Revolution in Philosophy*. Also available is A. J. Ayer (ed.), *Logical Positivism*, and Ch. 4 of *Philosophy in the Twentieth Century* by the same author. See also O. Hanfling, *Logical Positivism*, and the collection edited by Hanfling under the title *Essential Readings in Logical Positivism*.

Reading Guide to Chapter 4

The theme of this chapter was logic and scientific method. A. Flew in *Thinking about Thinking* has trenchant comments on ordinary reasoning and informal logic. R. Ackermann's *Modern Deductive Logic* is an approachable introduction to formal logic, or see R. C. Jeffrey, *Formal Logic: Its Scope and Limits*. W. V. Quine's *Methods of Logic* is authoritative, as is his *Encyclopedia Americana* article 'Logic, Symbolic', reprinted in his *Selected Logic Papers*. He provides an illuminating essay on the subject in his *Philosophy of Logic*.

If the paradox of Achilles and the tortoise interests you, then see some of the extensive literature on this in Wesley C. Salmon's (ed.) *Zeno's Paradoxes*, or A. Grünbaum, *Modern Science and Zeno's Paradoxes*. See also Ch. 2 of Salmon's *Space, Time and Motion*. An entertaining book on paradoxes is *What is the Name of this Book?* by A. Smullyan.

J. Burnet's *Early Greek Philosophy* still provides the best and clearest account of the ideas of the Presocratic philosophers, or see G. F. McLean and P. J. Aspell (eds.), *Readings in Ancient Western Philosophy*.

The best introduction to modal logic is G. E. Hughes and K. G. Cresswell, *An Introduction to Modal Logic*. On the subject of relevance logic, see A. R. Anderson and N. D. Belnap, Jr, *Entailment*, Vol. 1, or R. Routley *et al.*, *Relevant Logics and their Rise*, although it should be said that these are not books for the novice. The subject of counterfactuals was considered by David Lewis in his book *Counterfactuals*, and the variety of logics is explained and discussed by Susan Haack in her *Philosophy of Logics*. See also her earlier book *Deviant Logic*.

For a textbook introduction to the subject of possible worlds, see *Possible Worlds: an introduction to logic and its philosophy* by R. Bradley and N. Swartz. The controversy is well represented in L. Linsky (ed.), *Reference and Modality*.

The subject of probability is considered in R. Carnap, *The Logical Foundations of Probability*, 2nd edn, and the problem of induction more generally in N. Goodman, *Fact, Fiction and Forecast*.

For a general overview of the philosophy of science, see A. F. Chalmers, *What is this Thing called Science?*

Popper's views on the problem of induction were published in *The Logic of Scientific Discovery*, and his more recent ideas are to be found in Ch. 1 of *Objective Knowledge* and in *Conjectures and Refutations*. See also I. Lakatos and A. E. Musgrave (eds.), *Criticism and the Growth of Knowledge*. On the philosophy of science in general, see W. Newton-Smith, *The Rationality of Science*, and I. Hacking, *Representing and Intervening*.

For an account of the position taken by the logical positivists of the Vienna Circle, see A. J. Ayer's classical presentation in *Language, Truth and Logic*, or his helpful brief account of this in *The Revolution in Philosophy*. More recently, he has documented the movement and subsequent developments in *Philosophy in the Twentieth Century*.

5 Talking about Things

*Without sensibility no object would be given to us,
without the understanding no object would be thought.
Thoughts without content are empty, intuitions without
concepts are blind . . . The understanding can intuit
nothing, the senses can think nothing. Only through
their union can knowledge arise.*

— Immanuel Kant, *Critique of Pure Reason*

There is, then, the world of facts, of happenings and of things. But
my own direct observations confine me to a minute corner of this
rich world of objects and incidents. From this corner, do I see language, words, talk and reports as constituting a bridge or a barrier
between myself and the universe that consists of everything there is
or that occurs? And from this point of view, while it may be reports
of what is happening in China or Afghanistan that first strike me as
problematic, I can see that similar doubts may apply to reports about
what is happening nearer to home, or indeed anywhere outside the
time-space I currently occupy.

So what other people may tell me is of first importance to me. But
other people, together with their reports, lie on the far side of this
bridge or barrier of linguistic communication. (If I can cross it, it is
a bridge; if it remains impenetrable, it is a barrier.) To accept the
reports of other people, then, and so to enlarge immeasurably the
database of my knowledge, I must understand what language is and
how it functions. How do sounds that other people make, or marks
on pieces of paper, visual shapes in print or ink, or vibrations deliberately set up on the air-waves, become invested with meaning? And
how is communication between language-users possible?

Language, I know, has been a dominating interest of recent philosophy, both in the English-speaking world and also in many countries of Western Europe, where reflection on the structure of the system of signs that constitutes language is of as much interest for psychology, anthropology and literary criticism as it is for philosophy. Broadly, in the English-speaking world, philosophy has either concerned itself with the painstaking analysis of philosophically crucial terms commonly used in ordinary language – in particular, words like 'knowledge' and 'truth' – or it has been concerned with the construction of artificial logical languages, divorced from natural languages, and consciously freed from the untidiness and *ad hoc* qualities of ordinary speech.

But the questions I want to ask are not to be answered in either of these ways; for my questions are about language itself. My primary interest must be in language as report, together with the questions about meaning and reference that this involves, since it is through this that I can extend my knowledge of what there was, is, or might be. Language as communication or as a tool for social interaction is wider than this; but to understand this, too, I must have some idea of where and how language and reality meet. But relevant to *this* question is an understanding of how the ability to use language comes about. So I may also ask, How are language skills acquired? And what is it to be a competent language-user?

The acquisition of language

I begin, then, from the assumption that my views about the purposes language serves, and about its relation to reality, are conditioned by the way in which I think it comes about. Naïve theories of language learning start with the child wanting to convey meaning by naming objects – 'Mama', 'spoon' and so on. Children learn such words, it is sometimes assumed, because their elders point at the objects concerned, accompanying their pointing with the utterance of the object's name. This so-called 'ostensive definition' is opposed to verbal definition – definition, that is, in the way dictionaries do it, by an alternative turn of phrase – which, of course, is only possible when someone already has command of the language being learned.

These verbal pointings, though, can work only if a child has an intuitive grasp of the way that utterances even as simple as these are able to function as something more than mere grunts or babblings. A dog, by contrast, will never find a bone because a human finger is helpfully pointed in the bone's direction, nor can it be tempted by a verbal promise of 'bone tomorrow'. Children seem to grasp easily how to add verbs to the limited vocabulary of nouns with which they may start; to form plurals; to add adjectives and so on. They then go on to use language not simply to manipulate other people, for the satisfaction of their needs, although this may be the originating impulse, but also to express ideas.

I might compare this prior grasp of the principles of language to the way in which a child might discover logical or mathematical facts or principles. Perhaps someone else *hands* them to the child ready-made, but then the child will only accept and understand what it is being told if it is already capable of assimilating the logical or mathematical points itself; alternatively, the child might invent or construct them itself – rather as the twelve-year-old Blaise Pascal (1623–62), French philosopher and mathematician, was said to have been found secretly working his way, unguided, through Euclid's mathematical discoveries. But then, this is 'construction' in a special sense: the child is not free to create these logical or mathematical structures just as it likes.[1] Similarly, in the case of language, there is striking originality and creativity about young children's language learning; at the same time, there is an equally striking uniformity or conformity in approach.

But all these are contentious claims, and it is issues like these that lie behind the debate about the origins of linguistic competence which centres on the work of the American philosopher and linguist, Noam Chomsky (b. 1928). Something of this background, and of the views of the main protagonists in this debate, is already familiar to me; but nevertheless it is a contrast worth setting out.

Chomsky traces his philosophical ancestry to Descartes, to Leibniz and to seventeenth- and eighteenth-century grammarians who explored the notion of a universal grammar.[2] His primary debt, though, must be to Plato, whose Theory of Forms or Ideas was a theory about the universal terms – 'red', 'hot', 'equal', 'pretty', for example – that constitute a large part of talk about things. It was Plato who argued that we need, in some sense, a prior idea of equality in order to recognize *as* examples of equality the approximate instances of equality that are all we are actually likely to meet with in experience.

This idea that we face the world with preconceptions and preformed dispositions appears in theories of language as the idea of a universal grammar. The contrast implied by reference to a *universal* grammar is with *particular* grammars – the grammars people are taught if they are learning a second or third language, or studying the syntax of their own. A universal grammar corresponds, rather, to the grammar they need to grasp in order to acquire their *first* language in infancy. There may be alternative ways of explaining any features that languages have in common. For example, it might be that in prehistory humans shared a common language. But since no one, whatever his level of intelligence, is unable to come to terms with his own first language, it seems that the common elements amongst the Babel of world languages might more plausibly be explained by the rationalist hypothesis that they consist of structures which the human mind is peculiarly fitted to grasp.

Chomsky's work is an exploration of this 'deep structure' of language underlying its surface structure, and he argues that its accessibility to human beings reflects the fact that it is in some sense innate in them. Unlike the old theories of innate ideas, Chomsky's is a scientific rather than a logical or metaphysical theory. The disposition he has in mind is one that is genetically or biologically predetermined. As he puts it, the characteristics of language he has discovered are, if true, empirical facts, but they are a priori for the organism. His is a theory about language acquisition, then, which conflicts with the empiricist view that what people know they must have learned or acquired entirely from the environment. It is no accident, then, that Chomsky has taken issue on this subject with the behaviourist psychologist, B. F. Skinner (b. 1904), as well as with other philosophers of language in the empiricist and positivist tradition.[3]

Skinner takes the view that the acquisition of language can be explained in terms of conditioning: that humans learn language through a process of stimulus, response and reinforcement as these occur in a normal child's environment. These, he believes, set up linguistic habit structures: networks of association, fabrics of disposition to respond. Chomsky's view is that overt happenings like these, together with crude notions of stimulus and reinforcement, cannot provide a full account of how the ability to use language originates. He offers the example of an extraterrestrial observer who embarks on a scientific study of human beings – a Martian, for example, who knows both the English language and physics. The Martian, Chomsky suggests, would be unable to tell simply from what he could see that, while physics required generations of genius to develop, the mastery of English comes naturally to any child exposed to the language. As for terms like 'stimulus', 'response' and 'reinforcement', Chomsky argues that these are ambiguous and undefined when they are used in relation to human learning. They *may* be strictly defined, but in that case they will apply only within the laboratory and to simple organisms. Outside the laboratory they no longer function in a scientific and unambiguous way. It is not possible, then, in Chomsky's view, to extend the use of terms like these outside the laboratory, and certainly not to apply them to the complex enterprise of learning a natural language.

One feature of language which accounts for the difficulty of explaining it in these narrow and closed ways is that it is essentially open-ended. A small input is sufficient to give a child the capacity creatively to produce an indefinite number of completely original sentences, as well as to understand indefinitely many new sentences never encountered before. Hence the term 'generative' grammar. So Chomsky concludes that language is fitted to the human mind in a way that physics, for example, is not. In the case of language, he says, 'intrinsic principles of mental organization permit the construction of rich systems of knowledge and belief on the basis of scattered evidence'.[4]

Many of the observations of Ludwig Wittgenstein (1889–1951) in his *Philosophical Investigations* can be interpreted as showing just how scattered the evidence is on which people base their grasp of linguistic rules. Take, for example, the following passage:

> . . . A writes series of numbers down; B watches him and tries to find a law for the sequence of numbers. If he succeeds he exclaims: 'Now I can go on!' – So this capacity, this understanding, is something that makes its

appearance in a moment. So let us try and see what it is that makes its appearance here. – A has written down the numbers 1, 5, 11, 19, 29: at this point B says he knows how to go on. What happened here? Various things may have happened; for example, while A was slowly putting one number after another, B was occupied with trying various algebraic formulae on the numbers which had been written down . . .

Or again, B does not think of formulae. He watches A writing his numbers down with a certain feeling of tension, and all sorts of vague thoughts go through his head. Finally he asks himself: 'What is the series of differences?' He finds the series 4, 6, 8, 10 and says: 'Now I can go on.'

Or he watches and says, 'Yes, I know *that* series' – and continues it, just as he would have done if A had written down the series 1, 3, 5, 7, 9. – Or he says nothing at all and simply continues the series.[5]

These may seem enigmatic observations, but if one compares this to the case of a child learning language, it is clear that the ability to 'go on' in the case of language is even more puzzling than the ability to 'go on' in the arithmetic case. And yet the facility resembles the last two examples, rather than the first. It is this uncanny facility that Chomsky draws attention to, and it is this that an explanation in terms of stimulus and response misses.

Chomsky's solution, then, is to posit an innate capacity. Wittgenstein himself, however, offers a different explanation in the *Philosophical Investigations*. But his account of how language happens is also at the same time a theory of meaning, and in order to consider this and other theories of meaning, it may be useful to turn from the question of the origins of linguistic competence to more direct consideration of language itself.

The place to begin may well be with a distinction originally put forward by the Swiss linguist Ferdinand de Saussure (1857–1913). Saussure, who is the originator of the study known as semiotics, regarded language as a system of signs. The distinction he drew was between *langue* and *parole* – 'language' and 'speech'.[6] It is to *langue* as the underlying structure or sequence of rules involved in a language that both Chomsky's work and Wittgenstein's examples draw attention, and it is grasp of this that Chomsky describes as linguistic *competence*. At the same time, *parole* or 'speech' is what, without formulating rules, people, including young children, pursue in practice; and this Chomsky describes as linguistic *performance*.

Bearing in mind these distinctions, I see that my question initially must be at the level of performance or use. It is here that I must first seek to answer the question of meaning. Considerable light is thrown on this starting point, though, when I observe that the learning of language is a distinctive human capacity – a point only confirmed by the occasional instance of an intelligent higher mammal achieving some rudimentary concept of naming and sentence-formation. It is shaped, too, by my acceptance that grasping how to 'go on' as a language-user represents some kind of quasi-logical and intuitive leap. Given these two background assumptions, I am in a position to consider some of the accounts that have been offered of the relationship between speech and external reality. I am in a position, that is, to consider a question which I can provisionally pose as: 'What do words and sentences mean?'

The imagist theory of meaning

It would be natural to suppose that all words are used in a similar sort of way, and that this way is to *stand for* something. This assumption lies behind the naïve view of a child's early language learning, for example. The debate about language can indeed, historically, be looked at as a debate simply about what it *is* that words stand for. Early empiricist philosophers, in particular Locke and Berkeley, believed that words stood for ideas in the mind: an alternative view is that there is a one-to-one correlation between words and objects. So one answer to the question 'What does the word "moon" stand for?' is that it stands for the mental picture someone forms when thinking about the moon. Another is that it stands for the moon itself.

The first type of view was put by Locke when he spoke of a person using sounds as 'signs of internal conceptions' that stand as 'marks for the ideas within his own mind, whereby they might be made known to others'.[7] Berkeley, on the other hand, having endorsed Locke's correlation between words and ideas, went on to point out that objects themselves become redundant. Locke had spoken of matter as 'something I know not what', but Berkeley argued that since we neither do nor *can* know it, everything we want to take into account is encompassed within the two regions of (a) words and (b) the ideas in our minds (and God's) for which these words stand.[8]

But even without taking this further step, there are problems about taking mental entities as the subject-matter of language. For example, ideas in the mind are essentially private to each person. How can they be compared? Locke himself wondered how it would be if perhaps 'the idea that a violet produced in one man's mind by his eyes were the same that a marigold produced in another man's?'[9]

A prosaic answer to this question, but one carrying some weight, is that both men have a common physiology, and that therefore a similar cause would produce a similar effect. Perhaps I never *can* know that what I see as purple is not seen by you in the way that I see orange. But why should I suppose this? Better to assume – because it is the simpler hypothesis – that our experience is comparable and also that our language in describing it refers to something beyond the purely mental.

The issue is essentially this: the idea of mental entities as the subject-matter of language suggests that meaning is a three-termed relationship:

THOUGHT   LANGUAGE   THE WORLD

Meaning in this format is something in the consciousness of a speaker, which he expresses through the symbolic medium of language. Language itself here appears as something which is completely transparent. But structuralists like Jacques Derrida (b. 1930) have challenged this assumption, pointing to the obtrusive density of language, its use of metaphor and symbolism, particularly in literature.[10]

This is not the only reason, though, why I might want to reject this account of language. To begin with, the theory of the triple relationship would mean, I notice, that a mention of the word 'moon' would involve:

1. a mental image or thought:	2. what is said:	3. an external correlate:
the thought of the moon	'the moon'	the moon

I have already seen how an account like this might give rise to a temptation to dispense with the third element in this account. For Berkeley indeed took that step. I must now consider, though, whether another way of showing the triple theory to be wrong would be to show that the *first* element is eliminable. In other words, I must consider whether the relation between language and the world may not be, after all, in some sense direct. If so, then perhaps it is wrong to make a distinction between language and thought. Later, then, I must ask whether or not it makes sense to suppose that I engage in a *double* process, first thinking and then expressing my thought in language, rather than in a single process which has various manifestations. But first I must consider the other part of this possible trilogy of relationships: the relationship, that is, between language and the world.

The picture theory of meaning

If I focus on one particular use of language – that is, language as it is used to assert that something is the case – then I may become bewitched or entranced by a metaphor: the metaphor of language as a mirror of reality. I may believe that sentences represent a structural model, a picture, of the facts they describe. It is a theory of this sort, which he later came to reject *as* bewitchment, that Wittgenstein set out in his early work, the *Tractatus Logico-Philosophicus*.

There is a story that Wittgenstein took his image from a scale model of a car accident, assembled by the French police at their headquarters in Paris. The way in which the model cars and roads represented the crude fact of the accident seemed to Wittgenstein to provide a revealing metaphor of the relation between language and the world.[11] An alternative metaphor would be to say that language provides a map of the terrain of facts.

The theory itself, though, says nothing about how the human mind makes the connection between language and what it maps, and so the question of reference becomes a central concern. 'How does the word "car" represent a real car?' I might ask, looking at how the scale-model represents the car in the accident. I may feel I can answer this if, avoiding the complexities of the accident-scene, I limit myself to some simple spatial images: a rose, for example, lying next to a glove on a table. But what if I want to say there is no rose lying next to the glove? And no glove? And no table? What kind of picture of the facts would this be? Or if I want to make assertions about 'all' or 'some' roses? Or to indicate alternatives, as in 'Either it is a rose or a carnation'?

It might be said that all these are difficulties flowing from the inexactitude of ordinary language. Hence in the *Tractatus* the relationship implied may not be one between ordinary language and ordinary objects, but between the logical elements of language and whatever it is in the world that these elements indicate. An *ideal* language, it might be thought, should faithfully reflect the structure of the world. A *natural* language does not necessarily do this.

Whether in an ideal or natural language, though, this problem of reference is central to a 'picture' theory of meaning, and the idea that objects can be named and pointed at – 'ostensive definition' again – is a fundamental aspect of such a theory.

Meaning and reference

A referential theory of meaning, then, seems to carry with it a certain view of language learning. According to this way of explaining things, one might suppose that a child arrives in the world, and needs to come to terms with the surrounding language of his culture, rather in the way that a foreign anthropologist might arrive among a tribe speaking a totally unknown language. Foreign anthropologists, however, are assumed to know already what language *is*, and to be able to function efficiently in their own. They have only to grasp that when the native speaker points to a bush and names it, this is a well-understood and unambiguous procedure. They have a name for a bush in their own language and have simply to carry out a straight exchange of names. But it is precisely this kind of assumption that the American philosopher W. V. Quine (b. 1908) and other recent writers on reference cast into doubt, in the case of both the anthropologist and the child.

First of all, certain assumptions have to be made about conventions (like pointing) and about expectations (the desire to communicate on some particular basis and for some particular purpose). As far as the first is concerned, it might seem that someone could point, for example, to a flower, and say 'Flower' and be understood. But suppose the person is really pointing to one of its petals – or its colour – or its shape – or even its smell?

It also has to be assumed that both parties to this exercise of communication construe the world in the same way – see it as broken down into individual animals, or plants, for instance, within a wider landscape, rather than as patterns of colour and shape, or as animal/-plant parts, or animal/plant groups. The fact is, though, that there are cultural differences between peoples, even if not as striking as this: snow, for example, seems a single concept to a European, while an Eskimo, for whom such distinctions are important, will have a number of different words for snow and a number of differing concepts covered by these words. An Australian Aborigine may define many different kinds of blood relationship, while the modern European will take account, on the whole, of a more limited range of parents, children, cousins and similarly close relatives.

So reference in itself is not unproblematic. But suppose one *could* point unambiguously at something; suppose, that is, that naming is not quite such a hazardous procedure as these considerations suggest. In this case, the different question arises: what is the *content* of a name? In particular, is it a certain description, no matter how brief? Or are names essentially devoid of descriptive content?

It was Frege who originated the modern debate on this question with his seminal distinction between meaning as Sense (in German, *Sinn*) and meaning as Reference (*Bedeutung*).[12] He pointed out that when people made the (empirical) discovery that the Morning Star was in fact also the Evening Star, they were noticing that the two different phrases – Evening Star and Morning Star – while their Sense was different, had the same *Reference*; the two phrases were in fact two different descriptions of an identical physical object. So, for Frege, as well as the sign, or name, 'Morning Star' and the Reference – the star itself – there is also the Sense of the sign – in this case, the star that appears in the morning.

But Frege's Sense (*Sinn*) was not a mental entity, like the 'ideas' of Locke and Berkeley. It was potentially something in the public domain, even though different people might use two different expressions to refer to the same object. Frege gave as an example of this a Doctor X who might be known to one man simply by his date and place of birth, by another simply as currently living in some particular place.

Proper names, then, seem at first sight to need both a Sense and a Reference. Frege's examples seemed to show that objects cannot simply be verbally pointed at. A word which expresses this notion of verbal pointing is 'denoting', and it was in a famous paper with the title 'On Denoting' (published in 1905)[13] that Bertrand Russell argued that a distinction should be made between the *grammatical* subject of a sentence and its *logical* subject, and that a definite description of the form 'the so-and-so' should be analysed so that the apparent subject becomes an element in the predicate. For example, 'The author of *Waverley* was S' should, Russell argued, be seen as involving three separate claims: (a) that at least one person wrote *Waverley*, (b) that at most one person wrote *Waverley* and (c) that whoever wrote *Waverley* was S.

This kind of analysis offers a way of dealing with the problem touched on in the last chapter – the problem of referring to non-existent entities. Russell took the sentence

'The King of France is bald'

and suggested that the grammatical subject of this sentence,'the King of France', is not its *logical* subject. So the sentence does not really refer to a non-existent King of France at all. Its correct analysis according to Russell is:

1. At least one thing is King of France
2. At most one thing is King of France
3. There is nothing which is King of France and is not bald.

So expanded, it turns out that 'the King of France is bald' is a complex assertion which, because its first element is false, can itself be unproblematically taken as false. (The alternative, as the last chapter showed, might have been to attribute some kind of shadow existence, or subsistence, to the non-existent King of France.)

The point of this analysis was to reduce, rather than add to, what we claim to know. For, Russell believed, 'Every proposition which we can understand must be composed wholly of constituents with which we are acquainted.'[14] In the case of a proper name, like Julius Caesar, for example, we can talk about Julius Caesar but we do not *know* him in the sense of being directly acquainted with him; so Russell believed that our reference must be to things we *are* acquainted with, in this case the elements of some description of Julius Caesar, not Caesar himself.

Russell's argument, then, virtually dispenses with naming, since it seems that in principle any content or meaning in an apparent subject-term can be transferred to the predicate by this analysis, leaving only an empty pointing-word as a logical subject. Later, Russell was prepared to say: 'The only words one does use as names in the logical sense are words like 'this' or 'that'.'[15] As for the predicate terms, Russell saw these as pointing-words, too, in a different way. But in their case, he believed they pointed to universals of the kind Plato had postulated in his Theory of Forms.

Russell's elimination of the grammatical subject is continued in the work of the American philosopher, Quine, who has offered the idea of a language freed from referring expressions. Or, in Quine's words: 'Whatever we say with the help of names can be said in a language which shuns names altogether.'[16] In Quine's example, instead of saying 'Pegasus exists' and so referring to an imaginary horse, one might say 'something Pegasizes'. Similarly, to be Socrates is to Socratize. Proper nouns become verbs; logical subjects become predicates.

The British philosopher Peter Strawson (b. 1919) has remarked on these suggestions that people would not be able to learn the Russell/Quine language unless they had mastered the ordinary language. And, indeed, it is tempting to suppose that there must be more to proper names than this.

But if there is more to proper names than this, it would have to be some kind of descriptive content. Arguments of Saul Kripke (b. 1940), however, demonstrate the difficulties involved in taking proper names to have any single or unique descriptive meaning or content. For example, William Shakespeare is widely known as the author of *Macbeth* and certain other plays. But it seems to make sense to say that Shakespeare himself might not have written these plays at all; they might, perhaps, have been written by Bacon. And

Shakespeare himself might have spent his time in some quite different way. If this were so, it seems unlikely that anyone would insist that Bacon *was* Shakespeare on the grounds that 'Shakespeare' must be the name of the author of *Macbeth* and other plays.

In ordinary discussion, there may be clusters of descriptions associated with a proper name, and no single description may be essential for identification. Kripke, however, believes that a proper name can, conventionally, be bestowed on someone in some agreed way – in the case of people, this might well be a matter of parentage and birth. Once a proper name has a fixed reference like this, Kripke describes it as a 'rigid designator'. And once something can be designated rigidly, in Kripke's view, other true descriptions can be found by following through causal links and connections. A non-rigid designator, by contrast, is a description which various individuals *might* fit, although only one *does* as a matter of fact. For example, 'the Governor of the Bank of England in 1984' is a non-rigid designator.[17]

Why should there be this reluctance to accept that names amount to descriptions? I can answer this question by considering what I would have to say about language if names *were* nothing other than abbreviated descriptions – if, that is, there were no points where language touched reality. No matter how consistent it might be, a free-floating structure of linguistic practice would be simply that. A usable structure cannot be free-floating. It must have at least some anchor-points in the ground of reality. For these anchor-points, proper names and the objects to which they belong seem the obvious first place to look. The alternative is to say that my talk refers only to what is in my own mind – meanings 'in the head' – the 'psychologistic' view that Frege was first concerned to attack. A story to illustrate the problem was constructed by the American philosopher Hilary Putnam (b. 1926). His story of Twin Earth may be told thus:

> 'Twin Earth' is closely similar to our own – its inhabitants even speak English – except in one respect. This is that the liquid in the rivers, oceans and seas, which falls there as rain and which Twin Earthers drink and find thirst-quenching, is not H_2O, but a different chemical compound, XYZ. Twin Earthers, however, call it 'water'. Now if a spaceship from Earth were to visit Twin Earth, the

occupants might at first suppose that 'water' has the same meaning in both places. When they discover the chemical difference, though, they might report: 'On Twin Earth the word "water" means XYZ.'

But suppose that chemical analysis were for some reason impossible – suppose, perhaps, that the comparisons could have been undertaken in 1750 – then the difference would not be discovered, nor would the difference in meaning.

The moral to be drawn from this story is that if meanings are confined to what is in people's heads, it would have to be said that the Earthers and the Twin Earthers had a common concept of water, since for most people in either world the mental image or concept of water is based on its surface characteristics, not its chemical structure. But in Putnam's view, at the time when he devised this story, this would be false, since they are talking about a quite different chemical substance. And by the criterion of chemical structure, the meaning of 'water' is *not* the same in both places[18]

Putnam's story, then, is designed to support the view that meaning must be pinned down in some way to what is external – the world without rather than the world within. This is a so-called 'realist' view of meaning, to which an anti-realist might reply that the Earth explorers were warranted, or entitled, to describe what they found as water.

But Putnam argued that this is not either our common-sense or our scientific way of proceeding. What 'natural kind' a thing is, is a matter which present or future investigation might determine differently. The reference of 'water' is in some sense established independently of the views of particular groups or individuals at particular times.

As far as water is concerned, Putnam's story seems unconvincing. Ice is frozen water; steam is vaporized water; but is it still water after freezing or vaporizing? I do not know how to decide this. But a different example – an example of a different 'natural kind' – could have convinced me. Perhaps on Earth electrons are fundamental particles, while on Twin Earth whatever plays the electron-role is a composite of other particles. In a case like that, I think that I might follow Putnam and deny that there are any electrons on Twin Earth.[19]

I might prefer to do this rather than abandon the idea of objective meanings. For suppose I *were* to abandon the idea that objective meanings can be found across social groups and cultures; suppose, that is, that I were to seek for an explanation of language entirely in terms of what words mean to the people who use them, in the context in which they employ them.

In Putnam's story, his two earths are not self-contained. His space-ship occupants make comparisons about language-use. Although only one language, English, is involved, the example would work in the same way if the Twin Earthers spoke French or German or, indeed, some completely unknown language of their own. But the very idea of translation between languages has been undermined in two very different ways. The logician's attack is concerned with problems of meaning and reference; while what might be called the 'social observer's' attack is conducted on a very wide front indeed. The 'wide front' would include Marxists, who hold that language itself is a product of social conditioning and class-consciousness, and social relativists – people, that is, who believe that standards of truth and morality are internal to a particular society – including those influenced by the findings of anthropology and linguistics. They would include, too, philosophical sceptics about meaning like Feyerabend who have propounded an extreme version of the doctrine of 'incommensurability' between languages.[20]

Problems of translation

The logicians' attack is exemplified in the work of Quine. Quine specifies two particular difficulties: the first, the problem of translation either within or between languages, which he calls the lexicographer's problem; the second, a grammarian's problem essentially connected with the notion of what counts, in a language, as a significant sequence of sounds.

        1. The lexicographer's problem is that, since he is unable to say what 'meaning' is, he deals only in the concept 'alike in meaning', that is, synonymy. But the notion of synonymy itself, in Quine's

view, defies analysis, except in terms of meaning, so the would-be lexicographer is trapped within a circle he cannot escape.

2. The grammarian's problem is that, faced with determining what it is to 'have meaning', he must deal in the concept of significance. He must try, that is, to determine what word-sequences are significant. The problem, though, is that the class of utterances studied by the grammarian is infinite. It is impossible as a matter of fact to describe all possible meaningful utterances. (And the converse difficulty, a sentence containing a nonsensical string of sounds, can be intelligible if the nonsense is put in quotation marks; for example, ' "Oompa-do-pa" is meaningless'.) This means that the grammarian is not even free to *discard* any sequences of sounds, in order to approach his task of classification the other way round – that is, by saying what *cannot* be included rather than what can. And so, in Quine's view, the notion of grammar as straightforward description of what can be said in a language is mistaken.

Quine's sceptical conclusions extend to encompass a thesis of the *indeterminacy* of translation: this is that, in effect, no matter how much we might be able to find out about the behaviour of a group of people speaking an alien language, there is an indefinite number of ways of interpreting what they say. In other words, many systems of translation, internally consistent but incompatible with each other, would fit with that information.[21]

A yet more radical claim, though, is that language can only be learnt from 'inside' by a native speaker. This is the thesis of *incommensurability* – the thesis that one cannot measure what something means in one language against what it means in another; they just cannot be compared. It is a thesis closely connected with anthropological, cultural and social theories. For anthropologists, the problem of *Verstehen* (understanding) has been familiar since the work of Wilhelm Dilthey (1833–1911) and Max Weber (1864–1920). A common example is that of the Azande and their belief in witchcraft. Anthropologists have argued that it is not possible to understand the Zande theories of witchcraft except by entering the Zande way of life and using their language.

A different, and equally famous, example of a radical restructuring of reality and language was offered by Benjamin Lee Whorf (1897–1941) on the basis of observations of the Hopi Indians in North

America. While the claims made have been disputed, the Sapir—Whorf hypothesis, as it has been called, is important in showing what *might* be meant by such a claim, whether or not it is actually borne out in this case. Whorf's claim was that the Hopi Indians had no notion or intuition of time; that their language contained no words or constructions referring to past, present or future. Nevertheless, he claimed, their language was able to give a complete picture of their experience. At the same time, it conceals, he suggested, an alternative metaphysic, just as does our own view of static space and flowing time. Our own metaphysic is based on seeing the universe under the two great cosmic forms

SPACE   and TIME

The Hopi metaphysic, by contrast, sees the world under the division:

MANIFESTED and UNMANIFEST

The manifested consists of everything that is or has been revealed to the senses, so it includes our present and past, while the unmanifest includes all we would call future as well as everything mental. Within the Hopi framework, expressions of space and time are avoided by using expressions of extension, operation and cyclic process.

Edward Sapir (1884–1939) summed up his own conclusions from such findings in these terms: 'The fact of the matter is that the "real world" is to a large extent unconsciously built up on the language habits of the group. No two languages are ever sufficiently similar to be considered as representing the same social reality. The worlds in which different societies live are distinct worlds, not merely the same world with different labels attached.'[22] Later, he wrote: 'Such categories as number, gender, case, tense . . . are not so much discovered in experience as imposed upon it because of the tyrannical hold that linguistic form has upon our orientation in the world.'[23]

But can language really have such an effect? It is hard to imagine what it would be to be liberated from this tyranny – even more to be liberated from the tyranny of the 'hardest' of categories, that of logic. And yet, in *The Idea of a Social Science*, Peter Winch (b. 1926) wrote: 'a knowledge of logical theory will not enable you to understand a piece of reasoning in an unknown language; you will have to learn that language'.[24] Winch himself was strongly influenced in his thinking by the later Wittgenstein. The theory of language that

Wittgenstein advanced in *Philosophical Investigations* and in later works, has been summed up in the slogan 'meaning is use'.

Language-games and the 'use' theory of meaning

The central idea of Wittgenstein's *Investigations* is that the question of what words *mean* is to be answered by seeing what they *do*. In this view, social context, intention and function are the keys that unlock language. To understand these, the unit of meaning must be, as Frege first argued, whole sentences, not words taken in isolation.

Single words can themselves function as sentences, though, and indeed this happens in Wittgenstein's first simple model of what he calls a 'language-game'. In this model, two builders use a language consisting of the four words 'block', 'pillar', 'slab' and 'beam'. When the first builder calls out 'block' the second builder brings him a block which he has learnt to bring just at that call. Understanding this language, for its two users, is to be able to engage in routines like these. Or, in this primitive language-game, as in more complex ones, the meaning of an utterance is its use.[25]

The minimum number of people, though, who might construct a language (or, in Wittgenstein's terminology, play such a language-game) would be two. Empirically, occasional examples of, for example, a wolf-child – a human baby fostered by a wolf – seem to bear this out. Language neither appears nor persists in conditions of prolonged solitude. It is not necessary, though, to base the philosophical argument on such disputable empirical grounds. Instead I can ask: what would it be to create a private language – a language which only I can understand? I might think I could do this perhaps by keeping a secret diary. But how would I know that the secret mark I put down on Wednesday referred to the same sensation I had associated with that mark on Tuesday? What would it be to make a mistake? And if it is not possible to make a mistake, then the concept of getting it right cannot get any purchase. Of course, I can rely on memory; but, as Wittgenstein says, this is like someone buying several copies of the morning paper to confirm that what he reads there is true.[26]

The 'use' model of language, then, is essentially social. Its implication is that there is no one answer to a question like 'What do words mean?' And in favour of this view, one may recall the many other diverse functions of language apart from naming: words can, for example, be used to express surprise, to make promises, to threaten, to describe actions, to flatter, to assent, to dissent and so on. So, to see what any particular word means, it could be argued that it is always necessary to embed it in an utterance, to become aware of the intention of the speaker – including his beliefs, wishes and desires – and to understand the role that the speaker's utterance plays in a particular social and cultural context.

To emphasize intention and communication in this way is to recognize the nature of language as an institution or, as the American philosopher John Searle (b. 1932) describes it, as a rule-governed form of behaviour. In the hands of ordinary language theorists like J. L. Austin (1911–60), it is by finding out how a word or a sentence functions in a rich variety of contexts that illumination is to be found – the kind of illumination that a general formula cannot supply.

Does this mean, then, that understanding an isolated utterance is dependent on understanding an entire social context – the 'language-game' of which that word or sentence forms a part? Contemporary followers of Wittgenstein have pursued this line of thought to the conclusion that even within an individual language there are self-contained 'forms of thought' (the languages or 'language-games' of religion, for example, or science or poetry) which do not intersect, cannot be translated into each other's terms, and have their own criteria of truth and falsity. This parallels the case of translation between different natural languages – if one were, for example, to come across some lost tribe speaking a hitherto unknown tongue – where the claim is that, since culture is expressed in its language, learning the language could only be done from, as it were, the inside.

Is everything, then, relative? Does everything that is said depend for its meaning on who says it? Are words not capable of providing a common currency between human beings? Are there no common ideas which cross the boundaries of race, culture, social class, location in time and place? When I consider these questions, I am inclined to accept the importance of social context in explaining some aspects of an individual's language and orientation to the world. But I cannot *generalize* this notion without making it incoherent. A generalized and universal relativism in the end obliterates the distinction between what someone intends to say and what he actually does say. And even to interact for minimal purposes, this is a distinction it has to be possible to make. Without it, language is reduced to the mere making of noises.

But insistence that there must in the end be, in some sense at least, a direct relation between language and the world is not incompatible with also recognizing the connection between meaning and use. I cannot free myself from the notion that the possibility of using language successfully actually depends, in fact, on there being a correspondence between words and things, or between sentences and states of affairs. But at the same time, the question of how words come to be understood may be better answered by looking at the part they play in many kinds of social interaction. The alternative theory, though, continues to 'bewitch' with the thought that language must, after all, in some sense be a map if it is to be a guide. Or, as Putnam expresses this: 'Talk of use and talk of reference are parts of the total story.'[27] It is because I believe *this* that I can also believe that my picture of reality can be deliberately distorted by the language of others who desire to mislead. Or, in brief, it is only because I believe in truth that I can also believe in lies.

Notes to Chapter 5

1. See J. Piaget, *Structuralism*, pp. 61–2. While some of Piaget's conclusions may be contentious, he has established experimentally that children reject at one stage in their development logical or mathematical truths – for example, conservation of quantity – which will strike them as obvious at a later maturational stage. For Piaget's account of the development of children's logical and mathematical understanding, see J. Piaget, *The Language and Thought of the Child*.

2. For an account of this historical background, see N. Chomsky, *Cartesian Linguistics*. The most straightforward brief account of Chomsky's own views is Part 1 of *Problems of Knowledge and Freedom*. His considered philosophical position is set out in his *Language and Mind* (enlarged edition, 1972) and *Reflections on Language*. See also J. Lyons, *Chomsky* and J. J. Katz, *The Philosophy of Language*.

3. See in particular N. Chomsky (1964), 'A Review of B. F. Skinner's "Verbal

behaviour" ', in J. A. Fodor and J. J. Katz (eds), *The Structure of Language* (1964) pp. 547–79.

4. N. Chomsky, *Problems of Knowledge and Freedom*, p. 45.

5. L. Wittgenstein, *Philosophical Investigations*, para. 151.

6. There is a good exposition of Saussure's thought in J. Sturrock (ed.), *Structuralism and Since*. This includes also essays on Lévi-Strauss, Barthes, Foucault, Lacan and Derrida.

7. J. Locke, *Essay concerning Human Understanding*, Book III, 1, 2.

8. Berkeley's theory of perception was put forward in his *Three Dialogues*. The participants in the dialogue are Hylas, representing the materialist viewpoint, and Philonous, representing the idealist view which is Berkeley's own. This view was summed up in the phrase '*esse est percipi*' ('to be is to be perceived') – a brief way of saying that all our descriptions of objects involve reference to our own ways of perceiving or experiencing them.

9. Locke, op. cit., Book II, 32, 15.

10. Derrida's work is discussed in J. Sturrock, op. cit., Ch. 5. See in particular J. Derrida, *On Grammatology*. Derrida draws his inspiration from the work of the phenomenologist Edmund Husserl (1859–1938). His *Speech and Phenomena* (1967) deals with Husserl's theory of signs. For an American perspective on Derrida, see R. Rorty, *Philosophy and the Mirror of Nature*.

11. L. Wittgenstein, *Tractatus Logico-philosophicus*. For discussion of the *Tractatus* and the picture theory of meaning, see G. Pitcher (ed.), *Wittgenstein*, and Rush Rhees, *Discussions of Wittgenstein*.

12. G. Frege, 'Sense and Reference', in *Philosophical Writings*, trans. P. T. Geach and M. Black.

13. B. Russell, 'On Denoting', *Mind* 1905, reprinted in *Readings in Philosophical Analysis*, ed. H. Feigl and W. Sellars. It is interesting to compare the 'Waverley' example as presented in 'On Denoting' (1905) and in B. Russell, *Introduction to Mathematical Philosophy* (1919), p. 177. In one case the example used is 'The author of Waverley is Scotch'; in the other 'Scott is the author of Waverley'. Subsequent discussions have created another variation: 'The author of Waverley is Scott'. I have preferred an ambiguous abbreviation.

14. B. Russell, *The Problems of Philosophy*, p. 58. Ch. 5 of this book sets out Russell's views on knowledge by acquaintance and knowledge by description.

15. B. Russell, *Logic and Knowledge* (ed. R. Marsh) p. 201.

16. W. V. Quine, *From a Logical Point of View*, p. 13.

17. For Kripke's views, see S. Kripke, *Naming and Necessity*, or his 'Identity and Necessity' in S. P. Schwartz (ed.), *Naming, Necessity and Natural Kinds*.

18. H. Putnam, 'The meaning of "meaning" ', in *Mind, Language and Reality, Philosophical Papers*, Vol. 2. Putnam later abandoned the view

that the meaning of 'water' (a 'natural kind' term) could be pinned down in this way, but not the idea that language must somewhere be anchored in reality. See in particular 'Reason and Realism', in *Meaning and the Moral Sciences*.

19. I am indebted to Peter Forrest for this example.

20. See P. Feyerabend, 'Against Method, a Defence of Anarchy', in *Minnesota Studies in the Philosophy of Science*, IV, ed. M. Radner and S. Winokur.

21. See W. V. Quine, *From a Logical Point of View*, Ch. 3. See also 'Mind and Verbal Dispositions', in S. Guttenplan (ed.), *Mind and Language*, p. 90. In *Word and Object*, Quine does not claim that all individual sentences are indeterminate in this way: he speaks of 'stimulus meaning' in the case of simple sentences expressing common sense-experiences, e.g.: 'This is red.'

22. From E. Sapir, 'The Status of Linguistics as a Science', *Language*, Vol. 5, pp. 207–14; quoted in G. Sampson, *Schools of Linguistics*, p. 83.

23. E. Sapir, 'Conceptual Categories in Primitive Languages', *Science* Vol. 74, p. 578; quoted in Sampson, op.cit., p. 83.

24. P. Winch, *The Idea of a Social Science*, p. 135.

25. L. Wittgenstein, *Philosophical Investigations*, para. 2.

26. See L. Wittgenstein, op.cit., paras. 243–363. In 'Can there be a private language?', A. J. Ayer challenges this position with an account of Robinson Crusoe on his desert island. Crusoe *could*, he believes, name objects – both external objects like birds flying overhead, and also internal states like headaches or pains. When Man Friday turns up, Ayer argues, there will be difficulty in principle in Crusoe conveying both kinds of meanings to him, although clearly it will be easier to make him understand the first than the second. A. J. Ayer, *The Concept of a Person*, pp. 36–51.

27. H. Putnam, *Meaning and the Moral Sciences*, p. 100.

Reading Guide to Chapter 5

An excellent introduction to the philosophy of language is Ian Hacking's *Why Does Language Matter to Philosophy?* More technical and detailed expositions are D. Cooper, *Philosophy and the Nature of Language*, and B. Harrison, *An Introduction to the Philosophy of Language*. On language acquisition, see P. Fletcher and M. Garman (eds.), *Language Acquisition*.

For Chomsky's position, see initially Part I of his *Problems of Knowledge and Freedom*; then, to set the debate in a historical context, his *Cartesian Linguistics*. For Chomsky's more recent views, see also *Rules and Representations*. For further discussion of the relationship between logical form and deep structure, see D. Davidson and G. Harman (eds.), *The Semantics of Natural Language*. Skinner's general position is to be found in his *Beyond Freedom and Dignity*.

Useful brief discussions of the work of Lévi-Strauss, Barthes, Foucault,

Lacan and Derrida are to be found in J. Sturrock (ed.), *Structuralism and Since*. For an excellent and clear exploration of the implications of structuralism in various areas of human thought – biology, mathematics, language, literature – see J. Piaget, *Structuralism*.

For discussion of the problems encountered by the empiricist philosophers in connection with ideas, concepts and language, as well as their general philosophical theories, see J. Bennett, *Locke, Berkeley, Hume*.

G. Sampson in *Schools of Linguistics* offers a readable and comprehensive account of problems of meaning and translation, including the social anthropological issues mentioned here.

There are good discussions of Wittgenstein in both B. Harrison and I. Hacking.

Kripke's views are presented in *Naming and Necessity*, and are commented on by Dummett in his *Frege* and in *Truth and other Enigmas*. See also D. Wiggins, *Sameness and Substance*. For a general introduction to the work of Dummett and Davidson, see M. Platts, *Ways of Meaning*.

On natural kinds see the articles gathered in Schwartz (ed.), *Naming, Necessity and Natural Kinds*, particularly that by Quine.

6 Thinking about Minds

. . . to every rational being possessed of a will we must also lend the Idea of freedom as the only one under which he can act . . . we cannot possibly conceive of a reason as being consciously directed from outside in regard to its judgements.

– Immanuel Kant, *Groundwork of the Metaphysic of Morals*

I find, then, that language starts from what is – what exists – and is itself part of that external reality. The fact that it can distort that reality is no more than a necessary aspect of its capacity, on occasion, to reflect it. If I am satisfied that this is the nature of the link between language and the world, then I am in a position to turn my attention back from what is outside myself to what is most essentially inner: thought itself. But I cannot separate consideration of thought from consideration of whatever it is that thinks, reasons, reflects.

If it is this that I now want to consider, I can do it in one of two ways: (a) by introspection – taking my own mental processes and states as objects of scrutiny; or (b) by looking at the behaviour of others, since that is all that other people reveal to me. 'Behaviour' here can include *verbal* behaviour; 'others' can include non-humans, both animals and artefacts: machines, computers, cybernetic systems.

Introspection sounds the more limited strategy since it does, after all, confine me to a sample of one. But all the same, it is the more immediately compelling. Once again, I find I am looking inwards, but this time, perhaps, I can say that what I am looking at is not 'myself', but my Self. I may at first unreflectingly suppose that this Self is a kind of ghost that resides in my body, the source of thinking, feeling and awareness – what, if I doubt the reality of the soul, I would be inclined to call my mind.

Qualities of mind, in particular thought and reasoning, together with the language in which they are expressed, have long been taken as the defining features of the human being. 'Man', said Aristotle, 'is a rational animal.' This is more significant than that he is a feather-less biped, has hands, uses tools, important though all these characteristics may be.

But the role of introspection may be limited. If I subtract the *language* of thinking, which, as I have seen, is potentially in the public domain, is there anything left as thought? Can there be an unex-pressed thought, or is thinking, perhaps, silent speech? I remember that up to medieval times silent reading was an unknown art, and yet it is one now taken for granted. Perhaps silent speech is a similar skill of civilization and sophistication, and perhaps there is nothing more to thinking than the reduction of what is essentially overt and social to something less easily perceived. In this case, the Self may be nothing more than a certain flow of perceptions, for as Russell put it: 'When we try to look into ourselves, we always seem to come upon some particular thought or feeling, and not upon the "I" which has the thought or feeling.'[1] This is to echo Hume who wrote in similar vein: 'When I enter most intimately into what I call *myself*, I always stumble upon some particular perception or other.'[2]

It is striking to notice here how the empiricist tradition, continued from Hume through Russell to Quine and beyond, converges with the work of French structuralists like Michel Foucault (1926–84) in eliminating the notion of the self as the source of consciousness, the arbiter of meaning, the unifying *thing* that thinks. Foucault's remark that 'It is not man who takes the place of God, but anonymous think-ing, thinking without a subject'[3] sounds like an unconscious echo of Russell's statement in *The Analysis of Mind* that instead of saying 'I think' 'It would be better to say "it thinks in me" or better still . . . "there is a thought in me".'[4] And both these statements might be compared with the depersonalization of the *written* text – which is, after all, speech reified – that is a central feature of Derrida's philosophy of language. For Derrida, something written or pub-lished becomes a thing in the outside world, divorced from its originator, who has no better claim than anyone else to say 'what the author really means'.

Perhaps, then, I should consider whether the self is a myth which I may, taking my cue either from structuralists or from radical empiricists, eliminate by a better understanding of language. But whatever my ultimate conclusions, it seems clear that I must first attempt to answer some preliminary questions about the nature of *thought* if, as seems possible, it is thought that is the thread that can lead me to the elusive 'I'.

Thought and language

I may start here with the American philosopher Donald Davidson's (b. 1917) dicta that 'only creatures with speech have thought' and that 'a creature cannot have thought unless it is an interpreter of the speech of another'.[5]

Lying behind these remarks is the idea, not that thought *reduces* to speech, but rather that language and thought can both be explained only by reference to the setting of beliefs and desires in which they arise. The possibility of belief, though, depends on the possibility of being right or wrong: getting something right is essentially connected with being able to make a mistake. And for this concept, which is in effect the concept of truth, a shared language is necessary. Belief, then, in Davidson's view, is not intelligible as a private attitude, only as an adjustment to the public norm provided by language.

Two views in particular would run counter to this. I might say, 'Words can mean whatever I want them to mean.' Or I might say, 'Words can mean whatever *we* [i.e. members of my speech community] want them to mean.' Either of these positions can be described as an assertion of the indeterminacy of translation and the incommensurability of languages mentioned in the last chapter. For both suggest that what one person or group means by a word, or whole system of words – indeed, a whole language – may not be able to be reliably grasped and translated into other people's words or languages. But talk of indeterminacy of translation, if it is taken on an individual level as in the first case, amounts to the claim that a 'private' language is possible, and I have already seen the difficulties involved in this. Indeed, it seems in the end to be an unintelligible position, as Alice's pointed question to Humpty Dumpty in Lewis Carroll's *Through the Looking Glass* suggests:

> 'When *I* use a word,' Humpty Dumpty said, in rather a scornful tone, 'it means just what I choose it to mean – neither more nor less.'
>
> 'The question is,' said Alice, 'whether you *can* make words mean so many different things.'
>
> 'The question is,' said Humpty Dumpty, 'which is to be master – that's all.'[6]

Although Humpty Dumpty has the last word, it is a word which serves simply to reinforce the irrationality of his position.

The second, though, is a more plausible claim. For example, if educated users of English agree in using 'inchoate' to mean 'muddled' or 'vague', then sooner or later this will be added to the dictionary meaning of 'budding' or 'incomplete'. That is an example of a tacit change, unplanned and uncoordinated; but concerted overt agreement is possible, too, as, for example, in the way the convention has been established of using 'gay' to mean 'homosexual'.

Within any particular language, then, there is a certain partial, but not total, room for manoeuvre. Davidson accepts that a theory of language has to be relativized to a specific language, but rejects a full-blooded 'indeterminacy' claim like Quine's. So Davidson is right to say that: 'Sentences are true and words refer, *relative to a language*.'[7] On the other hand, his own view ties meaning to truth and both of these to the speaker's situation and context. It does this by means of a *formula* derived from a theory of truth established by the logician Alfred Tarski (1902–83). Tarski's formula, which was intended to apply only to formal or logical languages, was based on the idea that what, for example, makes the German sentence '*Schnee ist weiss*' true is simply that snow is white. The language for whose sentences truth is being defined is called the object-language. His formula, then, says of *any* sentence in a language that:

S is true if and only if p.

So, for example:

> 'Snow is white' is true in English if and only if snow is
> white

and

> '*Schnee ist weiss*' is true in German if and only if snow is
> white.

Tarski's so-called 'semantic theory of truth' is a powerful tool where
logical systems are concerned and, in spite of its apparent triviality,
it does explain how the concept of truth works.[8] Tarski's theory
assumes an understanding of meaning; Davidson, however, inverts
the procedure so as to take for granted an understanding of truth.

For Davidson, the rule for understanding the meaning of a sentence is simply this: give the truth conditions; that is, say what must
be the case if the sentence is to be true.

So Davidson's formula, described as the T-convention, is:

> (T)   S is T if and only if p.

Here, as in Tarski's formula, the sentence 'S' referred to says, with
some qualifications, that p. 'T' replaces 'true'. Because this is meant
to apply to natural language – language the way it is in fact used – it
is necessary both to specify *which* language it relates to, and also to
give details of context and setting. Observation then establishes in
any language what the truth conditions are, so that in the end, by
trial and error, it is possible to build up a system following the model
of the T-convention. (The test that a sentence has been correctly
understood will be that a native speaker of the language seems to
assent to it.)[9]

But Davidson's claim that questions of truth and meaning cannot
be taken in isolation from questions about the context in which an
utterance is embedded is more extensive than this. The context of
an utterance, for Davidson, includes details about the mental state
– beliefs, desires, wishes and intentions – of the person who utters
it. And these all feature in the explanation, not just of an utterance,
but also of an action.

So, to explain a simple *action*, that a man raised his arm, say, it is
necessary to state (i) what he wanted (for example, to attract the
attention of a friend), and (ii) what he believed (that this *would*

attract the attention of his friend). Just in the way, then, that I can interpret someone else's *action* only if I know the *reason* for it – that is, if I can give a forward-looking (teleological) explanation, rather than a backward-looking one – so my understanding of an *utterance* is incomplete unless I know something about the beliefs, desires and motives of the speaker. Of course, there is a public or objective meaning since, once someone has grasped this, he or she can take advantage of various possibilities of dishonest assertion – joking, exaggerating, lying and so on – which trade on the 'autonomy' of meaning. Taken together, however, these considerations suggest that the truth and meaning which are implicit in the public world of language are inseparable from the 'private' world of belief, intention and desire: in a word, thought.

If this is correct, then thought and language interlock. At first sight this would seem to confine both to humans, since humans are undisputed users of language. But only at first sight; instead of being restrictive, this stance could be enlarging. If I can attribute language to other living creatures, or if a computer can be programmed to engage in rational conversation, then the interdependence of language and thought may lead me instead to extend the attribution of thought, and therefore of mind, to them. But let me take these alternatives separately.

Dogs, dolphins and chimpanzees

Norman Malcolm (b. 1911) is not the only person to have owned a dog, nor the only one to have been impressed by his dog's mental capacities. But perhaps because he is a philosopher and a former friend and student of Wittgenstein, his dog's adventures are better known than most. Malcolm's dog is said to have barked up the wrong tree in pursuit of a squirrel. If a human were to make a comparable mistake, if would be natural to say, 'H *believes* that such-and-such.' In other words, a *thought* would be inferred. So much I can accept. But is attributing 'a thought' to a creature the same thing as attributing 'thought' to it?

Perhaps, witnessing a laboratory experiment in which pigeons are trained to take food from behind a particular door, it might seem natural for an observer, ignoring the more limited claims of the experimenter, to say 'The pigeon thinks there is food behind this door.' But then, outside the laboratory all living creatures, down to the common earthworm, take strategic action in their quest for food, safety, shelter. Why not describe all this as the entertaining of non-linguistic thoughts? The answer can only be that if I were to do so, I should have lost sight of the real difference between thinking and being, acting and reacting. I might even be obliged to extend my notion of thinking to the search of a plant for sunlight or the roots of a tree for water.

So I may decide that what I should look for instead, if I am to attribute thought to animals, is evidence of an intention to communicate. No doubt this happens more often than chauvinistic humans have in the past been prepared to grant. With either pity or contempt animals have been dismissed as 'dumb brutes'. But evidence of communication within species is increasingly impressive: dolphins have a communication system of their own which can without exaggeration be called a language; the frequency of notes in a bird-call has significance for other birds; there is a complex significance in the dance of bees; and many species have warning and mating cries that enable them to pass on simple information to other species members. Then as far as communication *across* species is concerned, dogs and cats appear to show understanding of human attempts to communicate subtle sentiments or even information. And chimpanzees brought up experimentally in a domestic situation have learnt the elements of human speech, using tokens or deaf-and-dumb language to compensate for the lack of the physiological apparatus of speech. Individual chimpanzees have shown they can form and express a concept of self, and also, having learnt how to convey true information, have used that capacity in order to lie.

Do these observations, then, show that the fact that animals cannot speak is simply a matter of the absence of such purely physiological requirements as larynx, lips and tongue? This would seem too great a claim, given the difference in linguistic capacity between even the best-trained chimp and the worst-trained human child. All the same, the difference might be a difference of quantity rather than of quality. I might agree with Quine here that what follows from the vastness of the language output of humans is not necessarily that there is a gulf between human and animal, but rather that the explanatory power of science is inevitably limited by the sheer complexity and volume of language.[10]

Nevertheless, if languages in any sophisticated sense are to be attributed to other living creatures, it has to be admitted that these languages would be truly incommensurable, beyond the way in which other human languages may be argued to be incommensurable. In relation to animal communication, the human is a Martian or extraterrestrial visitor, groping towards understanding. In Wittgenstein's famous aphorism: 'If a lion could talk, we would not understand him.'[11]

Davidson's view, then, which formed my starting point here, is better understood as the claim that only a creature with mastery of *human* speech can think. But can this limitation be justified? If animals can master *human* speech, then, I might ask, why not admit them to our speech-community with all that that implies? For even in the case of humans, this mastery of language must be thought of as potential rather than actual. The case of Helen Keller, who was born without speech, hearing or sight, shows that in the case of humans, ways can be found round purely physical limitations. But at the same time it also shows that there is a deeper capacity of understanding in a human being than in any other creature, which strongly recalls Chomsky's 'innateness' thesis. In the case of Helen Keller, there was a *content* to be conveyed by speech, which in the absence of speech could be conveyed by other systems of signs which themselves had to be established by mute and intuitive communication.

This explains, perhaps, why people are so reluctant to abandon the notion of the unexpressed thought, the words that, as novelists say, 'do not come easily' to the lips. Poetry, literature and art exist to give expression to what language in its more direct forms seems unable to convey. It seems, then, that I can distinguish thought from language in the sense that thought is what language seeks to capture or express.

But if language and thought are, after all, separable, there is no reason not to attribute limited capacities for thought and belief to other living creatures. It would be odd, then, not to attribute *intelligence* to creatures which both adopt problem-solving strategies and, moreover, may have their own language for communication within their species. 'Communication', after all, is not only a speech-related term. There can be mute communication between animals, and between animal and human, as well as between human and human. Can only creatures which have speech have thought, then? Where animals are concerned, it seems this is too rigid and immodest a claim on the part of humans. But what, then, of the case of machines?[12]

Artificial intelligence: computers and the simulation of mind

Thought and intelligence are, then, closely intertwined. Thought is, I may suppose, the capacity that intelligence displays. If some kind of intelligence can be created in a factory or laboratory I may look at the resulting artefact – computer, robot or device – and ask, does this machine think?

But is 'artificial intelligence' a contradiction in terms? If the machine, perhaps a highly sophisticated computer, 'thinks' in the way its inventor has enabled it to do, should I attribute this borrowed 'intelligence' to it? Should I attribute its inventor's powers of thought to it? If someone programmes the machine with objectives, should I then say that the machine has goals and purposes of its own?

In the early days of computer technology, it would have seemed obvious that these questions were to be answered in the negative. But as early as 1950 the British logician and mathematician A. M. Turing (1912–54) was prepared to express the confident view that, by the end of the century, people would have no difficulty in accepting that machines think, although by then both 'think' and 'machine' would no longer mean quite the same thing.[13] A new breed of super-computers seems to have brought us earlier than he had anticipated to the point Turing envisaged.

In order to understand how these facts relate to the questions I am asking about language, thought, mind and reasoning, I must know something of the goals of the originators of these machines. Clearly there is a difference between what might be called the instrumental-ist and the speculative reasons for attempting to create artificial intelligence – or even its more limited offspring, automated reasoning. The instrumentalist goal is the immediate practical problem-solving one that consists in devising machines specifically designed to fulfil a particular function – machines which may do the job, whatever it is, more adequately than a human being because they are more sophisticated, faster and tireless. The speculative goal has practical implications, too: it is speculative only in the sense that it is the goal of discovering more about human mental processes by attempting to imitate them in computer programs. In the end, though, the two goals of problem-solving and simulation overlap: in devising a machine to solve problems I throw light on how the human mind approaches that problem; in succeeding in simulating mental processes I provide a blueprint for the invention of problem-solving machines.

I want to know, then, whether there are irreducible differences between minds and machines – whether 'artificial intelligence' is ineluctably artificial. But I must be sure I am comparing like with like. Perhaps instead of comparing, in crude terms, minds and machines, I should contrast the hardware that houses the computer processes with the embodied brain, the brain that is accessible to the neurophysiologist and that houses, in some sense, human mental processes. And perhaps those processes themselves should be compared, not with the computer, but with its programs. If I make *these* distinctions and *these* comparisons, then I may find the parallel more plausible and less offensive than I might initially have supposed. Both human and computer processes may have in common structure and function. And as a result, the difference in the 'stuff' which makes the process possible may come to seem less important.

Of course, the hardware makes a difference to *some* aspects of a self that I may regard as mental. Just because it lacks an organic body, a computer is proof against sexual urges, cravings for food and drink or a desire to rest. Lacking a body, too, there are problems a computer finds difficult that I would find easy simply because my embodiment enables me to handle and manipulate objects: spatial terms are readily within my grasp, so that instructions which would be elementary to me may be beyond the grasp of, for example, an industrial robot.

But I know that many of the ways in which I think myself distinctive and the machine inferior are ultimately imitable by machines.

Programs may be written, for example, so as to leave some decisions open, to be taken by the computer at a later time, in the light of circumstances, or even to allow the computer scope to arrive, independently of human guidance, at new ways of making decisions. This means that a programmer cannot necessarily foresee everything that a computer will do. Nor is it the case that computers must work through all possibilities by the method of exhaustive search. Heuristic search theory provides general principles for making the exploration of possibilities systematic, so providing the kind of short-cuts in thinking that humans take for granted.

On the other hand, I can recognize some processes as peculiarly unsuited to computer programming. While task-orientated programs fit with the computer's problem-solving skills, it is not clear by *what* kind of program I could arrange for a machine to experience pain, or emotions, or see an after-image. It seems that the computer's world is the world of the cognitive, rather than the world of the affective – the imitation of human knowing rather than the imitation of human feeling.

But the fact is that whatever the success or failure, the attempt at modelling creates a new situation: the new aspect is that where previous reflections on the nature of human thought were no more than free-ranging speculation, these simulation attempts provide a *test* of the accuracy or inaccuracy of the theory behind the program. If the theory about a thought-process or piece of reasoning is correct, the program is usable. If not, not. And among the features that *have* been established in this way are some which are particularly relevant to my own inquiry.

First is the discovery of the way in which actual perception is conditioned by setting and expectations. I know that, where a machine is concerned, it is necessary to build in information about the 'frame' or setting within which any process is to take place – things which I can take for granted in human approaches to problem-solving. (In the human case, if I give someone a cake recipe, for example, I need not describe the kitchen and the oven.) Here, then, something must be explicitly *added* to a computer's information if it is to deal with a particular problem.

Conversely, in ordinary life, the mind is continually eliminating the irrelevant to hear what it wants to hear, see what it wants to see.

A human picks out the sound of English sentences from a hub-bub of noise, the shape of a familiar word from a careless scrawl. A machine is in the position of someone trying to pick out sentences in a crowded room where the speakers are using an unfamiliar foreign language. It needs to be told how to recognize patterns and how to eliminate the inessential. In general, what is usually taken for granted by humans has to be made explicit in computer programming.

Secondly, while the complexity of language and the difficulty of programming a machine to use language like a human being has become apparent, it seems significant that thought and reasoning can be translated into non-verbal, symbolic, and even pictorial or diagrammatic language. This strikes me more forcibly when I recall the problem that was faced by scientists who sent information into space in a search for other intelligence in the universe, and also that of others who left a buried capsule for our remote descendants to discover. In both cases, a common language could not be assumed, but the language of computers – numbers and diagrams – provided a realistic means of communication, a method of analogical representation. I know, too, that conversely there are areas of science and mathematics where debate, argument and progress can no longer be interpreted in verbal terms, but can be expressed only in terms of symbol and number.

Mind, matter and behaviour

I conclude, then, that in looking at thinking, I am looking beyond the purely verbal. I grasp this dimly when I envisage the possibility of intergalactic communication between intelligent beings; more concretely when for the sake of a computer program I attempt to express in diagrams or numbers what could more readily be expressed in words.

But is this, in the old terms of philosophical debate, a materialist view? Or does it protect the notion of the mental as something irreducible and untranslatable into materialist or mechanistic terms? One thing that the comparison has shown is that in a certain sense – or at least for the limited purposes I have in mind here – the matter–mind controversy is irrelevant. The constitution of the thing that thinks is not important if what I am interested in is the process itself.

But even this debate may be pre-empted if I find that the language of mental concepts is, after all, unnecessary for describing human experience. In *The Concept of Mind*, the Oxford linguistic philosopher Gilbert Ryle (1900–76) offered a complete analysis and explanation of mental terms – words such as 'know', 'believe', 'think', 'will' – in ways which referred only to overt behaviour – or at least to *dispositions* people might have to behave in certain ways.

Here I may compare the kind of behaviourism put forward by philosophers with that which some psychologists take as a background assumption. A philosophical or logical behaviourist like Ryle is trying to show how one might in principle dispense with mentalistic terms. It is part of his claim that there is no residue – nothing left unaccounted for. A psychological behaviourist, on the other hand, may merely be an agnostic about the mind. For methodological reasons, a psychologist may want to look only at what is measurable and observable. If there is a non-material mind, that is not his business. And in any laboratory experiments, the mentalistic stage in an explanation is, on a behaviourist view, simply redundant. For example, in the laboratory, the sequence:

deprivation of food → feeling hungry → eating

can be abbreviated without the loss of anything essential for research purposes to:

deprivation of food → eating

The psychological behaviourist may, however, draw stronger conclusions that this. B. F. Skinner, for instance, is clear about the implications for human thought: 'Human thought', he writes, 'is human behaviour. The history of human thought is what people have said and done.'[14]

But perhaps I should distinguish the question of how I can tell what people have thought or what someone now is thinking from the questions (a) of what it is *that* someone has thought or is thinking, and (b) of *whether* thought or thinking is something that occurs in distinction from overt bodily movements. Perhaps, too, I should, as in the case of computer programs, distinguish those which are questions about cognition from questions about other people's *feelings* – their pain, happiness, moods, level of consciousness.

In the first case, some kind of proposition always seems to be involved – a thought *that* something is the case. Or a hope that . . . expectation that . . . belief that . . . wish that . . . In the second case, no 'that' clauses are involved. A person simply *is* happy, sad, or in pain.

In either case, though, the behaviourist perspective seems to offer a truth about *my* access to what is, as one says, 'in another person's mind'. But it is also a truth about other people's access to what is in mine. And I know how easily I can trick, mislead or conceal, but also, even if I do none of these things, how prone *they* are to misunderstanding.

Ryle's thesis is aimed at exploding the myth of mind as another kind of existent, located in the body like a pilot in a plane or a driver in a car. It is based on analysing mental terms *dispositionally*: that is to say, by analogy with concepts like 'fragility' or 'malleability'. Instead of interpreting these terms as ways of describing an abstract characteristic inherent in, say, glass or wax, it is possible to see sentences using the terms as translatable into sentences saying what would *happen* under specified circumstances. To say something is fragile is to say that it will easily shatter if dropped or struck with a heavy object. To say that it is malleable is to say that it can easily be moulded, given the right sort of conditions.

Similarly, in the case of mental characteristics, to say, for example, that a girl knows how to ride a bicycle is not to attribute an abstract characteristic to her but to say that, given the right circumstances, she will successfully ride a bicycle. To say that a man wants something will be to say something about what he would do if offered it. To say someone hates someone else is to talk about the aversive behaviour he or she is likely to adopt if that other person is present. It seems it is *this* kind of analysis that the behaviourist is committed to, although no analysis like this can be entirely free from objection, and the task of refinement may be indefinite, given the number of qualifications needed to guarantee the truth of any particular translation. (I might have to add, for instance, that the potential cyclist does not consider it undignified, that the person who wants something is not an ascetic or a masochist, that the hater has no reason for concealment, and so on.) Nevertheless, there is a certain truth in the behaviourist's point, well expressed by Norman Malcolm in this way: in the case of another person, he writes, '*I see amusement in his face,* or *sullenness in his posture.* I am not compelled to infer these things from something else that I see.'[15]

I can see two main problems, though, with this position. One is that there are certain mental concepts it does *not* seem plausible to deal with in this way. How am I to account, for example, for reflective thought? Or the exercise of imagination? The other is the problem of transferring this, which is a good explanation of how I become aware of *other people's* mental processes, to my own case. For the fact is that I do not attribute mental happenings to *myself* on the basis of behaviour. I do not have two concepts of pain, one for my own case, the other for other people. It is true, though, that I verify 'I am in pain' differently from the way in which I verify 'he, or she, is in pain' or 'you are in pain'.

One solution to this problem might be to see 'I am in pain' not as a statement at all, but as the way in which other people have, on the basis of my behaviour in infancy, taught me to *express* my pain. Thus the problem of the asymmetry of meaning as between first-person and second- or third-person uses of mental terms might be overcome by showing that they are, as Malcolm suggests, 'linked in meaning by virtue of being tied, in different ways, to the same behavioural criteria'.[16]

Nevertheless, there is a crudity about the behavioural analysis of mental terms that I would still wish to avoid, and since there is, in any case, so large a part of my mental life left unaccounted for, I have to consider whether the psychological position linked with this kind of philosophical analysis is itself plausible.

I note that even Skinner, although a leading exponent of behaviourism, denies his intention to eliminate the private world of the mind. He writes: 'It would be foolish to deny the existence of that private world, but it is also foolish to assert that because it is private it is of a different nature from the world outside. The difference is not in the stuff of which the private world is composed, but in its accessibility.'[17]

In other words, behaviourism, whether philosophical or psychological, encourages me to recreate the world in terms of public observable events. If I ignore my own introspective experience, though, it seems I may find myself obliged, as one writer put it, to 'feign anaesthesia'. Skinner's claim is that private experiences cannot be discussed in public interpersonal language without misunderstanding. The goal of self-awareness – the instruction over the door at Delphi, 'Know yourself' – is set aside as a handicap to psychological investigation.

But the message of the behaviourist programme, however agnostically presented, is essentially materialistic. The subject to which it is appropriate to attribute behaviour is a physical object: the body. Other forms of materialism, though, attach more importance to the brain and nervous system of the body than to the crude overt movements of the whole mammal, bird or other living creature. Where views like these are concerned, it is the brain itself which thinks, feels, has sensations. But this approach is not necessarily hostile to behaviourism. Indeed, it may take the notion of *dispositions* to behave in certain ways as an intermediate step in telling a complete physicalist (i.e. materialist) story. For a disposition is more easily identified with a brain-state than is an actual bodily movement.[18]

From this point of view, then, the mentalistic terms of ordinary language are a heritage of 'folk psychology' – destined, like talk of witches or vital spirits, to fall into disuse with the advent of sophisticated enlightenment, or else to continue in use, in the way we continue to talk of the sun rising and setting, with no longer any thought that this implies the pre-Copernican view of the planetary system. Whatever language we choose to use, advocates of this view say, the facts are better explained by neuroscience; and the resolution of problems about minds is in the end empirical, not linguistic. As I have seen, it was a fault of a cruder form of philosophical behaviourism that it made it seem otherwise. Neuroscience, on the other hand, instead of merely offering an alternative vocabulary, has revealed much about the brain's microstructure that can affect my understanding of mental states and conditions. I know, for example, that these can be manipulated and affected by deliberate or accidental damage to the brain. I know that drugs and alcohol or the process of senile decay can affect rational thought; that a vast array of chemicals can affect the emotions; and that consciousness itself is affected by anaesthetics that act on the brain and nervous system, or by the cruder eventuality of a blow to the skull.

Does this mean, then, that sensations are simply processes in the brain? When I talk about recalling the scent of blossom, am I really talking about a neural happening? Is that recall itself a brain process? The possibility of identification may make sense by analogy with certain other scientific identifications: for example, I may initially be willing to accept the identity of a cloud with a mass of particles in suspension, or of lightning with an electrical discharge.

Nevertheless, although there is a sense in which these *are* indisputably identities, there is *another* sense in which this is *not* what a cloud is to me, nor what a flash of lightning is to me. In this sense, what the recollection of the scent of blossom is to me is not something that would yield to physiological inspection by a scientist with the means to observe my brain processes.

Perhaps, then, I should say that these are two ways of seeing the same thing? After all, I can observe a cloud or a flash of lightning either with the naked eye or with scientific measuring instruments. But in the case of human thought, is it 'the same thing'? And what would be the consequence of my thinking that it was? Would it, for example, simplify my approach to causal explanation where human beings are concerned? Or would I have destroyed distinctions which are necessary to my own self-concept – my own sense, that is, of myself as an agent, interacting with the world?[19]

Being a person

The problem I am now confronting is this: if cybernetic systems – robots and computers – can imitate human processes, and if it is only the complexity of the human brain that makes it harder to forecast and explain the behaviour of a human being than that of any other living creature, then it might seem that the most distinctive and valuable parts of human existence have been evaporated by a harsh and anti-humanistic science. Man is, after all, no more than a part of the nature he himself investigates. Or, as Derrida put it, these developments could be said to have a tendency 'to oust all metaphysical concepts – including the concepts of soul, of life, of value, of choice, of memory — which until recently served to separate the machino from man'.[20]

But is this necessarily so? At first, I may uncritically accept the mind–body dichotomy, seeing myself as essentially a mind which owns a body — after all, the notion of self-control is the notion of mind in control of body. But, then, I may notice that sometimes I have a notion of myself, my person, which lies outside both mind and body. I may decide to discipline my mind, as well as my body — to control my own thoughts and emotions.

This notion, though, is an odd one when I think about it. A person who is neither mind nor body — does this make sense? Better, perhaps, to say that a person is a unity which possesses both mental and physical attributes. Might there not be a distinctive notion of a person as someone who both does things which are indisputably physical, like eating and walking, and also does things which are mental, like thinking and feeling? P. F. Strawson (b. 1919), in putting a view like this, writes of a person as the subject to which are attached both person-predicates (predicates which imply the possession of states of consciousness) and material-object-predicates, which do not. An experience, he maintains, can only be identified as *belonging to* someone, and the concept of a person must be taken as a primitive unanalysable concept.[21]

I can see that both this theory and the straight materialist position can solve problems I might otherwise find troubling in relation to causality. If, like Descartes, I want to maintain a duality of mind and body, the mental and the physical, then I must confront, as he did, the problem of interaction between the two. How can something which is non-material bring about changes in a material body? For the latter, it seems that a full range of causal explanations is already available. Indeed, the problem might seem to be the embarrassment of causal explanations that are on offer. A neurophysiologist may want to explain one neural process by reference to a preceding one; a psychologist may look for an explanation in some immediate environmental stimulus; if the psychological tradition is Freudian, though, the explanation is more likely to be in terms of unconscious causes in early childhood. A sociologist, on the other hand, will offer collective rather than individual explanations in terms, perhaps, of social class; while a Marxist may appeal to inexorable laws of history.

In the end, a complicated series of reductions of one science to another – broadly, of sociology to psychology, of psychology to physiology and chemistry – may leave a materialist conception of human beings standing. Confident that this is so, the materialist may strongly reject the intrusion into this tidy universe of a non-reducible element: the mental. The distaste is well summed up in the phrase applied to mental phenomena of this sort by J. J. C. Smart. They are 'nomological danglers', as are the psychophysical laws which would be necessary to explain them.[22]

This is a plausible use of Occam's razor. (William of Ockham (Occam) (c. 1285–1349) was a fourteenth-century logician who enunciated a fruitful principle of frugality in reasoning: that one should not multiply entities needlessly.) However, the contrary view has difficulties, too, as Socrates showed when, in the *Phaedo*, he argued that an explanation in terms of his body – its muscles, bones, flesh, skin – would totally fail to explain why it was that he was sitting in prison awaiting death, rather than hiding away in a hospitable foreign country. The reason Socrates himself gave for being there was *honour* – a different order of explanation altogether. It is different, first, in that it points forwards rather than backwards, and secondly, in that it posits a novel form of motivation – moral motivation.

So does the fact that human actions need to be explained in terms of what a person wants and is trying to achieve make the case of humans irreducibly different? Or can intentional human behaviour be explained and predicted in the same way that other phenomena are? Is man a subject for science, or a 'law unto himself'? The problem is that human acts are part of the natural order, but nevertheless it seems that they cannot be brought under deterministic laws. A person very often appears to have a choice as to what to do.

In addressing questions like these, Donald Davidson concludes that forward-looking explanations – explanations in terms of intention or reasons for acting – are not a different form of causal explanation from others. He reaches his conclusion, which he describes as 'anomalous monism', by insisting that what we deal in are not mental states or processes but *events*. And in the case of events, it is easier to talk of an identity between the mental and the physical. Mental characteristics, he believes, may be supervenient on (arise out of and be dependent on) physical ones, though not reducible to them.

Davidson holds, then, that a psychological explanation is an explanation that someone acted in a certain way because he had certain desires and certain beliefs. But although this is a causal explanation, he thinks there are no strict laws relating the mental to the physical. They would require too much detail and it would be too complicated to settle that some particular action would be the outcome in any particular situation. Nevertheless, the events that we are relating in terms of psychological phrases like 'believe', 'wish', 'hope' and so on, are, according to Davidson, also physical events, and as *physical* events subject to *physical* laws.

Do moves such as these towards a materialist perspective mean, then, that the apparently distinctive features of human beings are in the end to be subsumed under general causal explanations? And if so, must I lose my grasp on the mental which seems to be the seat of my commitment to reason and thought, as well as to the world of feeling, sensibility, emotion and the real power of the will? Would this mean, too, the loss of the notion of objective truth, which has allowed me so far to reject some ideas and directions as false, and to follow others fruitfully?

Pondering these questions, I am struck by an interesting, though frequently unremarked, feature of the identity thesis – the thesis, that is, that identifies mind with matter. This is that, like any authentic assertion of identity, it may be read in reverse. But if I invert the reduction

MIND - DISPOSITION TO BEHAVE - PHYSICO-CHEMICAL STATE

then the significance of the identification – the message that it apparently carries – seems to change. I find, then, that some physico-chemical states, those associated with living beings, and *possibly* with some artefacts of human making, are, at the level of the organism or object, to be identified first with behaviour but in the end, by virtue of their structure and the functions that they serve, with mind.

In other words, to reduce the mental to the physical is also to elevate the physical to the mental. At the same time it is, it must be

admitted, very much to enlarge the scope of the mental. Nevertheless, such a reconstruction means that I can now, finally, set aside
as idle the argument about the 'stuff' of things. And I can now ask,
'What, within *this* framework, does distinguish the human person?'

Rationality, freedom and will

Three things in particular seem to me important: these are rationality, will and creativity. Animals, too, show motivation which is
not directed simply to the satisfaction of bodily needs. They, too,
demonstrate curiosity (in humans the spring of intellectual inquiry),
a desire to explore and to have new experiences. But although these
characteristics are present in rudimentary form in other creatures,
the difference in degree between humans and the rest of nature is so
great as to be in effect a difference in kind.

Perhaps it is because of this effective difference, though, that
humans are also capable of love, self-sacrifice, spite, revenge, the
impulse to be creative and – as the example of Socrates showed – to
guide their own conduct by moral considerations.

It is this, in particular, which seems to fit most awkwardly with the
materialist hypothesis. For moral agency and moral responsibility, it
seems that freedom to choose – not to be bound by a network of
extraneous causes – is essential. Freedom seems, I might say, incompatible with a close mesh of causality. But having glimpsed some of
the layers of apparently conflicting causal explanation, the threat of
the causal nexus impinges less immediately. And the fact that the
'mental' is no longer outside this network, but integrated within it,
removes the sting.

For the freedom that I need may be only the freedom that lies
within my own hands – the freedom to 'be myself'. Perhaps freedom
in the case of any living creature means simply that the causes of its
behaviour lie within rather than wholly outside that creature. (But
this provides the cut-off point where machines would have to be
refused a place in 'our' universe – their existence and functioning
are a product of wholly external causes.)

For myself, I know that what I am is dependent on innate or genetic
factors, combined with present and past environmental influences.
Nevertheless, I know that these two elements – or indeed the first

alone – make the pattern of my being unique. Nature *always* breaks the mould after creating an individual. (*I* cannot be, I might reason, less distinctive than my fingerprints or voiceprint.)

Given this consideration, a metaphysical hypothesis about the 'stuff' of the universe or of human beings cannot deprive me of the freedom which is manifested in rationality, will and creativity. 'Both the invention of the wheel', I might say, 'and the acceptance of moral guidelines for living are evidence against crude determinism.'

But if my own freedom and rationality are consistent with a cohesive and causally explicable universe in which mind and matter merge – a universe from which mind has not been expelled, but in which matter is not, as Berkeley put it, 'stupid, inert and unthinking' – then I am drawn irresistibly to recall the starting reflections of philosophy in which appearances were rejected, and the search was instituted for an underlying structure and reality – mind, soul, God or nature.

Notes to Chapter 6

1. B. Russell, *The Problems of Philosophy*, p. 50.
2. D. Hume, *A Treatise of Human Nature*, Book 1, 6.
3. M. Foucault, *The Order of Things*. Foucault was distinguished as a critic of Western intellectual traditions. He is perhaps best known for his studies of madness and of sexuality.
4. B. Russell, *The Analysis of Mind*, p. 18.
5. D. Davidson, 'Thought and Talk', in S. Guttenplan (ed.), *Mind and Language*, pp. 19 and 9.
6. Lewis Carroll, *Through the Looking Glass, and What Alice Found There*, p. 269. Lewis Carroll was also the logician Charles Dodgson, and in that capacity he wrote in his *Symbolic Logic*: 'The writers, and editors, of the Logical text-books which run in the ordinary grooves . . . take, on this subject, what seems to me to be a more humble position than is necessary. They speak of the Copula of a Proposition "with bated breath"; almost as if it were a living, conscious Entity, capable of declaring for itself what it chose to mean, and that we, poor human creatures, had nothing to do but to ascertain *what* was its sovereign will and pleasure, and submit to it.

   'In opposition to this view, I maintain that any writer of a book is fully authorised in attaching any meaning he likes to any word or phrase he intends to use' (p. 165, quoted on pp. 267–8 of *The Annotated Alice*).

7. D. Davidson, 'The Inscrutability of Reference', in *Enquiries into Truth and Interpretation*, p. 239 (my italics).

8. Tarski's semantic conception of truth was presented in an essay written in 1933 in Polish, published in English in 1944 as 'The Semantic Conception of Truth', in the journal *Philosophy and Phenomenological Research*. The paradox of the liar, mentioned in Ch. 4, is a semantic paradox. It is *linguistic* or *semantic* in that it consists of trying to talk about a system from within that system. Such paradoxes have in common the fact that they combine a claim about truth with self-reference. Tarski's theory offered a way out of this and other semantic paradoxes, in part by distinguishing sentences from names of sentences. See the account of Tarski in W. V. Quine, *Philosophy of Logic*.

9. For this theory, see in particular D. Davidson, 'Truth and Meaning', in *Enquiries into Truth and Interpretation*, pp. 23 ff.

10. See W. V. Quine, 'Mind and Verbal Dispositions', in S. Guttenplan (ed.), pp. 83–95.

11. L. Wittgenstein, *Philosophical Investigations*, II, xi, p. 223.

12. This is not a new controversy. Descartes believed that animals, lacking souls, were mere machines – *bêtes machines* – and that intelligent speech and action distinguish human beings from them. Julien Offroy de la Mettrie (1709–51) agreed with Descartes that animals are machines, but argued in his book *L'Homme Machine* (*Man a Machine*) that humans are not essentially different. They are machines, too, and it would be possible to manufacture a mechanical talking man.

13. See A. Turing, 'Computing Machinery and Intelligence', in A. Ross Anderson (ed.), *Minds and Machines*. Alan Mathison Turing (1912–54) was an English mathematician, a cryptographer during his war service, whose interest in symbolic logic led him to the theory of computing machines. The name 'Turing machine' is given to the concept of a machine which is completely self-contained in its procedures once it has been given unambiguous instructions.

   In a paper published in 1936, before electronic computers existed, under the title 'On Computable Numbers', Turing set out the nature and theoretical limitations of computing machines, although by the time he wrote 'Computing Machinery and Intelligence' (1950), he was prepared to argue that machines were in principle capable of fully imitating human intelligence.

14. B. F. Skinner, *About Behaviourism*, p. 117. B. F. Skinner is a behavioural psychologist who has sought to establish conditioning as the explanation for human and animal behaviour, and who regards it as an appropriate tool for political and social control. His novel *Walden Two* describes a society built on such principles; its distinctive feature is the way in which human beings are treated as manipulable by punishment and reward.

15. N. Malcolm, *Problems of Mind*, p. 101.

16. ibid.,p. 91.
17. B. F. Skinner, *Beyond Freedom and Dignity*, p. 101.
18. Quine, for example, holds that a behaviourist explanation is ultimately an explanation in terms of neural events.
19. For two classic defences of the Mind–Body Identity theory, see U. T. Place, 'Is Consciousness a Brain Process?', and J. J. C. Smart, 'Sensations and Brain Processes', in V. C. Chappell (ed.), *The Philosophy of Mind.*
20. J. Derrida, *On Grammatology*, p. 9.
21. See P. F. Strawson, 'Persons', in V. C. Chappell, op.cit.; or his *Individuals: an essay in descriptive metaphysics.* P. F. Strawson (b. 1919) is a British philosopher working in Oxford within the tradition of linguistic philosophy. He has been influential in promoting a return to metaphysics in the Kantian tradition.
22. J. J. C. Smart, op.cit., p. 161. Smart takes this term from H. Feigl who, in his paper 'The "Mental" and the "Physical" ', uses the term for the laws themselves.

Reading Guide to Chapter 6

A clear and interesting general introduction to the theme of this chapter, the philosophy of mind, is P. M. Churchland's *Matter and Consciousness. Mind and Language* (ed. S. Guttenplan) is an important collection of essays on these topics. For Davidson's views on philosophical psychology see his *Essays on Actions and Events.*

The classic statement of philosophical behaviourism is G. Ryle's *The Concept of Mind*, while a committed defence of psychological behaviourism is to be found in B. F. Skinner's *About Behaviourism* and *Beyond Freedom and Dignity.* See also his science-fiction novel *Wal en Two.* For general philosophical discussion of behaviourist assumptions in the social sciences, see Charles Taylor, *The Explanation of Behaviour* and *Explanation in the Behavioural Sciences* (ed. R. Borger and F. Cioffi). See, too, D. Dennett's *Brainstorms.*

On the mind–body theory, there is an important collection of articles in V. Chappell (ed.), *The Philosophy of Mind*, those by Place and Smart being of particular interest. See also, on mind and matter, the essays collected in A. Ross Anderson (ed.), *Minds and Machines.*

Two comprehensive books on artificial intelligence by philosophers are M. A. Boden, *Artificial Intelligence and Natural Man* and A. Sloman, *The Computer Revolution in Philosophy.*

On the question of analogies with animals, see the article by T. Nagel called 'What is it like to be a bat?' in his *Mortal Questions.*

A good starting point for consideration of the question of what it is to be a person would be B. Williams's essay 'The Makropolous case' in his *Problems of the Self.* Other important though difficult books on this subject are P. F.

Strawson's *Individuals: an essay in descriptive metaphysics* and D. Parfit's *Reasons and Persons*.

Free will is an ancient and much discussed philosophical problem. I have not attempted to expound the differences between determinists, compatibilists and libertarians in this chapter, but available literature is extensive. One clear and readable account of the issues is D. J. O'Connor's *Free Will*, while there is a useful selection of readings edited by Gary Watson under the title *Free Will*. Two essays which advance the debate to encompass current pre-occupations are 'Man as a subject for science' by A. J. Ayer in his *Metaphysics and Commonsense*, and 'From Hope and Fear Set Free' by Isaiah Berlin.

An inspiring, original and wide-ranging book in this area is *The Mind's I: Fantasies on Self and Soul* by Douglas R. Hofstadter and Daniel C. Dennett, which brings together, with commentary, extracts from sources which might otherwise be difficult to track down.

7 Seeing Further

> *Weary therefore of dogmatism that teaches us nothing, and equally of scepticism that promises us nothing at all, not even to rest in permitted ignorance; challenged by the importance of the knowledge that we need, and made suspicious by long experience with regard to all the knowledge that we believe we possess, or that offers itself to us under the title of pure reason – we only have one critical question left, by answering which we can regulate our future conduct: is metaphysics possible at all?*
>
> – Immanuel Kant, *Prolegomena*

The understanding I have reached, then, is that one of the great gulfs people have believed existed – that between mind and matter – is no more than a superficial crack on the surface of reality. As far as this is concerned, there is only one thing in the universe, not two. I leave it to physicists to define it further, and I know already, from what I have heard about the chemical basis of matter, that the results of their explorations will be subtle, surprising, and far removed from the mechanistic materialism of nineteenth-century science. Indeed, the speculations of the pre-Socratic philosophers seem closer to twentieth-century truth on these matters than the received opinion of intervening centuries.

The Greeks, I know, thought of the universe as consisting of endless transformations of material. Nothing, they believed, can come out of nothing; nor is it possible that anything that actually exists could cease to exist, for, as they said: 'it will always continue to be, wherever one may keep putting it'. Hence the attraction for them of religions like the Orphic one. Perhaps it is here, too, that Western philosophy in its origins touches the wisdom and lore of the East. According to the Orphic doctrines, and some Eastern religions, all existence is cyclical – a wheel of birth and death, with rebirth in other forms – as animals or other human beings – for those who apparently pass out of existence. The pre-Socratic philosophers, then, saw a need to account for the appearance of change, for change *is* essentially coming into being and passing away.

We think of this phenomenon as change rather than as cessation and commencement, because when we refer to change we refer to a single aspect of some continuing existent ceasing or coming into being – change made visible by a background which remains constant. So when a leaf changes from green to brown, only the colour and texture change – the basic structure of the leaf remains as it was. It is a small step from that observation to the idea that when the leaf itself seems to decay and pass out of existence, there is simply a redistribution in the atmosphere of the minute parts of matter which came together to create the leaf.

It is in this sense that philosophers like Parmenides believed that change is illusory and that behind the appearance of change there is a constant and undifferentiated underlying reality. While Heraclitus, widely seen as the opponent of Parmenides both in antiquity and today, was making not a different point but essentially the same point, with his doctrine of flux. Heraclitus' famous remark that it is impossible to step into the same river twice suggests that what strikes us as a continuing object is a matter of a certain relationship of parts which themselves have no permanence and which it is impossible to pin down.[1] Permanence itself is in fact constituted by the fleeting and impermanent.

It is interesting to notice how Greek atomists like Epicurus (341–270 BC) turned these ideas into theories which seem remarkably like the theories of modern science. (They appeared in poetic form in the work of the Roman writer Lucretius (c. 99–55 BC), who set them out in his long poem The Nature of the Universe, De Rerum Natura.)[2] The Epicurean theory answered the question of how the universe was constituted in terms of atoms continually in motion and constantly regrouping to form new but ephemeral entities. It was a materialism that left little scope for religion: it aimed to banish the fear of death by showing that death was indeed the end of life, and held that the gods or god, if existing at all, remained aloof and uninvolved in the affairs of humans.

Would these same consequences, I wonder, accompany a twentieth-century view of a basically homogeneous universe which is nevertheless a maelstrom of movement and change? Should I, if I believe that the apparent variety of the world is reducible to chemical combinations and reactions, dismiss the idea of God, despite the part this idea has played in human life? And if I have no notion of mind as separate, can I have no concept, either, of the soul? If mental and physical merge, what am I to say of the spiritual? What are the consequences of *this* for those aspirations to immortality that I and other human beings sometimes feel? And, finally, though perhaps most immediately important, what attitude should I have to the animal realities of pain, suffering and death?

As I reflect on these questions, I see that they can hardly be answered piecemeal or one by one. Both questions and answers present themselves only as part of a loosely woven tapestry. I know that in the history of philosophy answers to *these* questions have most strikingly been offered in great metaphysical *systems* – whole, rather than partial, explanations, which include a total reinterpretation of the crude facts of experience.

Finding one of these systems acceptable as an answer to my question – if this is to be more than a mere emotional response – may be less a matter of intellectual judgement than of intuitive grasp. As the French philosopher Étienne Bonnot de Condillac (1715–80) wrote: 'As for suppositions, the imagination makes them with so much pleasure and so easily. It is from such foundations that one creates and governs the universe. All this costs no more than a dream, and philosophers dream easily.' Echoing Voltaire, he added '. . . One ignores details, the things under one's eyes; one takes flight into unknown lands, and one constructs systems.'[3] But even at the beginning of my inquiry, I noticed that some kind of intuitive awareness was essential for answering questions that I listed then. Here again, though, I feel I need a mentor and a guide. And so I turn once more to Sophia; and in answer to my letter, she writes to me in these terms:

Fifth letter from Sophia

Dear Q,

I think at this stage in your quest you may be interested to hear of a tale told by Plato in the Republic[4] It is a metaphor which you may find fits your experience.

In Plato's story, a group of prisoners lie shackled in an underground cave. A kind of primitive cinema screen is placed in front of them on which the shadows of objects are discernible. They cannot see the objects themselves, which are behind the screen. The prisoners amuse themselves and keep themselves occupied by guessing what the objects are of which they see the shadows projected on the screen. Some of them, in fact, become very proficient at this. But one of their number succeeds in freeing himself of his shackles and, seeing a distant chink of light, manages with much hardship and effort to climb up from the cave and out into the world of daylight and sunshine. There for the first time he sees the real objects of which only the shadows were visible below, and he is struck by their beauty and luminosity.

I suspect this may be the kind of experience of illumination you have written to ask me about. But I should add, if you are affected by this story, that in Plato's account the prisoner who escaped and had this experience felt it his duty in the end to return to the cave and tell his fellow-prisoners what he had seen. But, of course, when he got back, no one would believe him – particularly as the bright light of the sun had dazzled his eyes, so that for a time he became rather stupid at the shadow-guessing game they all continued to play.

Perhaps, if you think about this, you may be a little wary of continuing your quest. I hope not. But, all the same, you may ask, 'What kind of experience is this glimpse of the sun? Is it something in line with the kind of discoveries I have made up to now – just a further, more advanced stage of inquiry? Or is it different in kind from the modest advances in knowledge I have so far made? Well, Q, my dear young friend, there is a description in a letter said to have been written by Plato of the kind of experience it might be: 'It is not something that can be put into words like other branches of learning; only after long partnership

in a common life devoted to this very thing does truth flash upon '
the soul, like a flame kindled by a leaping spark, and once it is
born there it nourishes itself thereafter.'[5]

This certainly sounds more like what you, Q, initially described
in your letter to me as intuition. It could even be called mystic
insight. Mysticism is not so foreign to the twentieth-century
philosophy as you might think. Compare, for example,
Wittgenstein's saying: 'There is indeed the inexpressible'. And his
enigmatic concluding remarks in the Tractatus: 'My propositions
serve as elucidations in the following way: anyone who
understands me eventually recognizes them as nonsensical, when
he has used them – as steps – to climb up beyond them. (He must,
so to speak, throw away the ladder after he has climbed up it.)'[6]

I think perhaps you are ready for this kind of illumination. So I
can only suggest you look at some of the great systems of
metaphysics offered by philosophers such as Spinoza, Leibniz
and Kant. I should like to be your guide in these matters, but have
to tell you that age and health seem likely to prevent me. Do not
worry about me, but if I am able I shall write to you over the next
few days with a few suggestions, telling you of directions which I
myself have found most helpful in these matters.

> Yours,
> Sophia

Sophia kept her promise and I heard from her twice more, once on
the Stoic system, and once on Spinoza (1632–77), before I heard that
she had died, a volume of Epictetus appropriately in her hand. The
words at which it was open:

> Was it then misfortune and unhappiness that the gods
> intended for us when they endowed us with reason? Did
> they want us to be miserable and spend our lives grieving?
> Imagine how it would be if everyone were immortal and
> nobody ever went away, but we all stayed tied to roots
> like plants. Should we really sit down and cry whenever
> one of our friends leaves us, and again, if he comes back,
> dance about and clap, like children?
>
> Surely it is high time that we grew up and reminded

ourselves of what we heard from the philosophers – if indeed we did not see that they were offering us a remedy for our pain when they told us that this universe is one city, and the substance of which it is constructed single, that it conforms to a regular pattern and the time must inevitably come for one thing to give place to another; that some things must break up and new things arise, some things remain static while others change. The world is full of our friends, first of all gods, and next after them men, united as they all are in one family by natural ties. Some must remain together, but others must go their separate ways. We should enjoy their company while we have it, but not be sad at parting.[7]

Epictetus (*c.* 50–*c.* 138) was himself a Stoic. As a freed slave in inhumane and barbarous times, he needed to find a philosophical stance or perspective which would be valid independently of external circumstances. He found this in the Stoic system. Sophia had obviously found his perspective illuminating, for she wrote to me in these terms:

Sixth letter from Sophia

Dear Q,

The Stoic system flourished in changing forms for many centuries in antiquity, and indeed you may be interested to know that I have heard rumours of attempts to revive it in a form adapted to the present day.[8] However that may be, in its original Greek form, when it was associated particularly with the philosopher Chrysippus (280–206 BC), it involved an ascetic way of life. When later it became a philosophy for Roman emperors, some of that asceticism was muted, although it still embodied an ethic of strong self-control. In its later form, it flourished in the first and second centuries AD and it is that form which was moulded by Epictetus, Seneca (c. 4 BC–AD 65) – he was Nero's minister – and the emperor Marcus Aurelius (AD 121–80).

You will remember that I mentioned Stoic logic briefly when I wrote to you on that subject. Probably, though, it is Stoic ethics rather than Stoic theories about logic or again about scientific or physical reality that you will think of immediately as Stoicism. As far as that is concerned, it centres on two things: inwardly it involves self-control and tranquillity, outwardly social usefulness – not just on a narrow or parochial front, but on the stage of the world, on which all human beings meet as equals. This ethical system is based on the belief that God makes everything what it is and maintains the basic harmony of the universe. 'God' means the ultimate cause and fabric of everything that exists – something that can also be called the Logos or reason of the world – order, destiny or the law of nature. The idea of order, I might say, is fundamental.

So, in the Stoic system, the universe does not run one way in time, as we tend to think. Time is just an aspect of things. Instead, it follows through a never-ending series of cycles. Each cycle (the word was periodos – the Greek for a circular route: the 'road around') begins with creative fire, and ends, too, with fire. Like time, space is also only an aspect of things. Because they believed this, the Stoics held that the universe was a sphere bounded by a spaceless void (on the principle 'no space without body'). Of the things within our universe, the Stoics saw a gradation of ways of existing: least animate would be rocks . . . then plants . . . then animals, which possess some rudimentary psyche or soul . . . and, finally, rational beings. These, possessing reason, possess a spark of the creative divinity of which they are part.

The Stoics would have answered your question about God affirmatively, though their assent might not mean what you take it to mean. But they did think that because most humans do believe in some way in God, it would be a denial of reason not to accept this – indeed, they believed that using reason is to believe in God. They even advanced various proofs of the existence of God, which the ancient Sceptics, like modern ones, set themselves to attack. One of these proofs was based on the beauty and functionality of the universe – what today would be called an argument from design. But their opponents, the Sceptics, stressed the dark side of life – the disasters that afflict the world from time to time. They preferred to believe that the universe simply happened, just as it is – that there is no grand design, or Grand Designer.

The Stoic answer to this problem of pain and human suffering was that the dark is needed to give form to the light, as in a painting: the whole, though, is perfect and harmonious.

If these arguments have a modern flavour, put it down to the fact that these are perennial problems for human beings, and that where problems of this sort are concerned, people have never achieved the kind of shared conviction or consensus that they have arrived at in some other areas of speculation. Nor has anything parallel to scientific method emerged for settling such questions, or even for deciding who is to count as an authority on such matters.

As for the Stoics, it seems that it was the belief in the harmony of the universe that made possible the way of life that they advocated: one of harmoniousness with the universe. They saw virtue as the ethical route to that harmony of spirit – and virtue included intelligence, courage, justice and self-control. I once read, you know, that some North American Indians held a belief rather like this. I do not remember the exact words attributed to them, but the saying was something of this sort: 'The truly brave man knows neither pain nor pleasure, fear nor joy, agony nor self-indulgence.' This sounds very like the famous Stoic apatheia, and reminds me, in fact, of Epictetus' aphorism: 'Those whose bodies are in good condition can endure heat and cold; so also those whose souls are in an excellent condition can endure anger, and grief, and great joy, and every other emotion.'[9] The early Stoics aimed at indifference to the accidents of life – to health, possessions and public reputation – but their successors came to accept that, while these goods should not be essential for inner peace and public service, nevertheless they were advantages in life.

What, though, I think you will find most significant and imitable in the Stoic doctrine is their belief in the brotherhood of persons – their belief that, whatever race or creed a person has, whether foreigner or slave or co-religionist or atheist, the divine spark unites everybody; that the moral law is the way in which the divine nature shows itself in human concerns; and that this provides a common moral structure for everyone in the world. Stoic duty, in other words, is the duty of a citizen of the world, not of one particular country; it is a duty to promote the well-being of all those you can affect. You may like to think about some of these ideas, and in the meantime I shall write to you soon about the theories of Spinoza, which are not so far removed from these ancient doctrines.

Yours,
Sophia

It was only a few days later that I received a further letter from Sophia – as it turned out, the last she was to send.

Seventh letter from Sophia

Dear Q,

It seemed to me that both the life and ideas of Spinoza might interest you. Spinoza was opposed to the religious dogmatism of his day, and I know that you, too, have set your face against dogmatism – belief, that is, that does not permit of questioning. Spinoza's own family had fled from persecution, first from the Spain of the Inquisition, then from Portugal. It seems an irony, then, that the Jewish community in Amsterdam, where Spinoza spent his life, rejected and indeed excommunicated him. He believed, you see, in the spirit of Judaism, but not in its narrow legalism and orthodoxy.

His is essentially an ethical philosophy. Like ancient Stoicism, it provides a way of life – or perhaps I should say an approach to life: a way of finding an attitude and response to the eventualities and contingencies of living.

You could say that the love of God underlay the whole system that he worked out, but this would be paradoxical, for the fact is that during his lifetime and after his death he was regarded by many as an atheist. Indeed, his Tractatus Theologico-politicus was published anonymously (in Amsterdam, 1670), and his Ethics only after his death. He lived according to his principles: he refused the chair of philosophy at Heidelberg which was offered to him, preferring to retain his philosophical independence by earning his living as a grinder of optical lenses, although in the end this probably contributed to his early death from consumption.

Spinoza took his starting point from Descartes. His first philosophical work was an account of Descartes' philosophy.[10] But where Descartes had depended in the end on a personal God to justify his claims to knowledge, Spinoza maintained an austerely impersonal concept of God, based on a geometrical and logical method of reasoning. His central theories are set out in his Ethics. There he deals with the most ultimate categories of metaphysics: substance and attribute: causation, freedom and necessity. The deepest metaphysical questions – those concerning God and creation, the freedom of the human will and the freedom of God, human immortality, mind and matter – are all dealt with here. Descartes, in his system of philosophy, had seen reality as divided into two irreducible categories, two ultimately disparate kinds of substance, thought and extension – the mental and the physical. But Spinoza argued that logic compels us to the belief that there can be only one ultimate substance, which is self-sufficient and uncaused. The reasons for this are complicated; what I can say briefly, though, is that Spinoza held that to understand or to explain anything, you must know what it essentially is, not what it just happens to be. But he argued that nothing 'just happens to be'. If you can't find an explanation in the nature of the thing itself, then you will find it in something else. In the end, though, only one thing (which must therefore include all there is) could be both a complete explanation (cause) of itself (the Latin phrase that Spinoza used was causa sui), and also the cause, in the more usual sense, of everything else (causa omnium rerum).

For this reason, Spinoza believed it did not make sense to suppose that there might be two self-contained substances in the universe; the hypothesis that there might be led to insoluble problems about the interaction between the two. For how could mind affect matter? Or matter affect mind? (I believe you mentioned that you had reached a conclusion rather like this yourself.) For Spinoza, then, thought and extension are not two different things, but two ways of thinking about the same thing. This single substance must be infinite – it cannot be bounded, since it is itself everything. It follows, then, that if God is defined, as in orthodox theology, as infinite being, then the single substance identified with Nature must also be identified with God.

It is, of course, an important aspect of Jewish and Christian religious thought that the creator is to be distinguished from what is created. But this notion of a separate and separable God has engendered many of the problems that beset theological orthodoxy, in particular the problem of evil. Not that it is only a problem for the religious. As I told you in my last letter, the Stoics had already recognized the need for some kind of explanation of pain and suffering. But there is a special problem for those who believe in a benevolent and all-powerful creator. For religious believers, faith strains at certain questions: Is there any answer to a child's meningitis? Or a baby tossed up in the air and caught on a soldier's bayonet?

This problem of pain and evil is also the problem of freedom – ours and God's. Part of the world's evil is a product of our freedom – and that that should inevitably be so is a restraint on the freedom of God – God could not both make human beings free and also make the evil that results from human freedom impossible. For Spinoza that was no problem: he believed that everything is necessary, pain as well as evil. Everything must be as it is. This leaves no room for any notion of free will either for ourselves or for God. So Spinoza's account neither demands nor allows for conventional free will, and the idea of a transcendent creator – a creator outside and apart from its creation – is a logical impossibility.

Spinoza offered an argument for this that a modern physicist might find understandable in other terms. He argued that changes and exchanges of matter can take place only within the system of nature – that the proportions of motion and rest must remain constant within the system of nature taken as a whole. The physicist might agree that the idea of the entire system being penetrated by energy from outside is incoherent. Spinoza's, though, was a logical rather than an empirical point: it does not make sense to speak of a totality, and then posit something affecting that totality from outside.

God, in the Judaeo-Christian tradition, is often conceived in this external role. But the idea of God simply creating, by fiat, an arbitrarily chosen world, which was only one of many possibilities, was, for other reasons as well, rationally repugnant to Spinoza. Much better conceive of a God constrained by necessity; better, too, to conceive of the world as rationally explicable, in the sense that everything in it is as it has to be – a world of which it is true that understanding any part can, in principle, lead to a complete understanding of the whole.

That God might simply have wanted to create the world would presuppose God had a need or a lack – something which again is an absurd hypothesis. An imperfect, insufficient or inadequate being is not what any of the world's major religions mean by God. And both Jewish and Christian thought has hinted at the idea that God's creatures are not external objects to their creator, in those many suggestions that God has direct access to our minds and thoughts. Consider, for example, this passage from Psalm 139:

> O Lord you have searched me
>   and you know me.
> You know when I sit and when I rise;
>   you perceive my thoughts from afar.
> You discern my going out and my lying down;
>   you are familiar with all my ways.
> Before a word is on my tongue
>   you know it completely, O Lord.
>
> You hem me in – behind and before;
>   you have laid your hand upon me.
> Such knowledge is too wonderful for me,
>   too lofty for me to attain.
>
> Where can I go from your Spirit?
>   Where can I flee from your presence?
> If I go up to the heavens, you are there;
>   if I make my bed in the depths, you are there.
>
> If I rise on the wings of the dawn,
>   if I settle on the far side of the sea,
> even there your hand will guide me,
>   your right hand will hold me fast.

> If I say, 'Surely the darkness will hide me
>   and the light become night around me,'
> even the darkness will not be dark to you,
>   the night will shine like the day,
>   for darkness is as light to you.
>
> For you created my inmost being;
> you knit me together in my mother's womb.[11]

But without a transcendent God, if there is religious truth, it can only be metaphorical – an illuminating picture or aid to understanding, rather than a literal explanation of the facts of change and existence. Faith and reason must, if Spinoza is right, be kept apart.

And yet, as I said, the path of Spinoza's reasoning could be called a route to God. There are two reasons why this is so. One is to be found in Spinoza's account of the human mind; the other in his account of truth.

The human mind, according to Spinoza, is a 'created, thinking substance', a thinking thing (ens cogitans). This characteristic is sufficient to give a permanency lacking to the body, which is a fleeting and perishing part of extension. The human mind, by contrast, is 'part of the infinite intellect of God'.[12] But it is not, as Descartes had claimed, something different and distinct from the body; indeed, it is a kind of mirror or reflection of the body – or, in a different metaphor, it is the form or shape of the body. As Spinoza himself put it: 'The mind and the body are one and the same thing, which is conceived now under the attribute of thought, now under the attribute of extension.'[13] He went on to say that: 'the decision of the mind, together with the appetite and determination of the body, are simultaneous in nature, or rather [that] they are one and the same thing, which, when it is considered under the attribute of thought and explained in terms of it, we call decision, and when considered under the attribute of extension, and deduced from the laws of motion and rest, we call determination.'[14]

This double-aspect explanation of mind and body is easiest to grasp in the case of sense-perception, where the effect of something physical – an external object – on the body is to produce an idea in the mind – something which is neither solely physical nor solely mental – or, if you prefer, something which is both of these things at the same time. Spinoza rated the kind of knowledge generated by sense-perception as, after mere dreaming or imagining, the lowest, most uncertain kind – what Plato called 'opinion'. He held that scientific knowledge takes us to a higher level of understanding, and that the highest level of all is a single unified system of interlocking ideas.

So by understanding what a person is, and understanding man's place in nature as a thinking being, one can begin to approach those important questions of human happiness and freedom which are the goal of so much of this kind of reflection. If you follow Spinoza, then this is to come to understand yourself and others sub specie aeternitatis.

I know that you cling to the idea of individual self-determination, so the complete determinism of Spinoza's system may not appeal to you. If you were to accept it completely, then that personal and individual perspective must ultimately vanish. But Spinoza himself provided a simile in a letter he wrote, which might help to make his perspective more convincing: imagine, he said, a parasitic worm living in the bloodstream and trying to understand and interpret its surroundings. The worm would see each drop of blood as an independent entity; it would not be able to recognize the part played by individual drops in the bloodstream as a whole – nor could it understand that the more significant unit is the bloodstream as a whole, rather than the droplets of which it is constituted. But even the bloodstream taken as a whole is inadequately understood until it is seen in relation to all the other fluids in the body and to the body as a whole. If as a human being, you see your body and the bodies of others as isolated independent entities, you are like the worm in relation to the drops of blood. You have missed out on the wider understanding which is the key to real illumination.

But I said there was another way in which Spinoza's theory could be seen as a route to God. This consists in the fact that Spinoza saw his theories about knowledge and truth as necessary for salvation and for happiness. In his system, the truth of an idea is a matter of its relationship to other ideas, a matter of fitting with the whole system. An illusion, for instance, would simply be an idea which does not cohere with everything else that is known. And a judgement of perception is false when it does not fit in with other judgements of perception. I said before that in our knowledge of things (in Spinoza's view), we can ascend from the common-sense level of knowledge which is characteristic of sense-perception, to the scientific knowledge which explains our perceptual observations, finally reaching a higher level of logic, science, or metaphysics which is capable of explaining the explanations of science itself.

Unlike Descartes, Spinoza thought that we could recognize clear ideas – if you remember, Descartes thought it made sense to conceive of the possibility of deception even where clear and distinct ideas were concerned, if there were a malignant demon with sufficient powers. Spinoza would not entertain such a hypothesis. For him, mathematics and logic provided the standard of indubitability. This explains his philosophical method, which I daresay you may find surprising – a deductive system, imitating Euclidean geometry, in which propositions are derived from axioms, using a limited number of primitive terms. The nature of Spinoza's system is such that only one set of necessarily connected propositions can be true, and, since they all interlock and are interdependent, it would be possible to enter the system at any point and work out the rest from there.

The distinctive feature of Spinoza's view of truth, then, is this: that, for him, truth is something that is grasped by thinking clearly rather than by seeing, touching or otherwise observing by the senses. It is possible to know things independently of experience, for experience is only partial. While truth, as Spinoza has argued, is interlocking – parts, only, may be grasped, but ultimately every partial truth leads to every other. Potentially, knowledge is of a totality – and a grasp of that, or even of an aspect of it, is not a matter of sense-observation.

Some would say that this search for infallible knowledge is doomed to failure because it is misconceived. They would say that knowledge is only of the particular, and is only yielded by the senses. That is why I suggested that the appeal of Spinoza's system to you must be, for want of a better word, an intuitive

*appeal. It is an example of what a metaphysical system can offer,
and I hope that you will be encouraged to explore further this and
other systems. But I know that the cast of your mind is empirical.
You have grown up in an age of technology and are accustomed
to thinking that science is the only sound source of both questions
and answers.*

*You are not, of course, alone in this, and indeed, as far as
philosophy is concerned, metaphysics has been an unpopular
study for most of the present century. The only article of faith
permitted to adherents of the positivist and empiricist philosophy
prevailing in the English-speaking world has been that
metaphysics is meaningless.*

*But you may find more inspiration in some of the ideas I have
mentioned than in that austere denunciation. I leave you to think
about these things. For myself, I think this is a time for me to
reflect on Spinoza's most famous statement: 'A free person thinks
of nothing less than of death, and the wisdom of such a person is
a meditation not of death but of life.'*

> *Yours,*
> *Sophia*

I was touched and, I must admit, wryly amused, to notice the way
in which Sophia had adapted the usual translation of Spinoza's
dictum, which appears to relate to 'men' rather than 'persons'. After
a while, however, I began to reflect on what she had written. I found
myself impressed with the theories she had described. But as she so
astutely observed, I cannot alter the temper of my mind. On the other
hand, I have seen, too, the limitations of empiricism. In sum, I feel
that the unsophisticated theories of the past, whether rationalist or
empiricist, are unlikely to offer me the complete understanding I
seek. It is time, then, to consider whether the illumination I am
seeking lies in the sophisticated developments of these positions to
be found in contemporary sources.

Notes to Chapter 7

1. See Ch. 4, pp. 72–104.
2. Lucretius, *The Nature of the Universe.*

3. Condillac, *Traité des Systèmes* (1749), quoted in R. J. White, *The Anti-Philosophers*, p. 44. The anti-philosophical tradition is marked by the presentation of ideas in terms which are comprehensible to the ordinary person, using the vernacular as opposed to formal academic language, or a foreign tongue understood only by an educated minority. 'Establishment' philosophers at first reject such contributions as damaging to their professional mystique. Historically, however, the anti-philosophers have outlasted their critics; it is, after all, a tradition to which both Descartes and Voltaire belong.

4. Plato, *Republic, Book VII.*

5. Plato, *The Seventh Letter*, in Plato, *Phaedrus and Letters VII and VIII.*

6. L. Wittgenstein, *Tractatus Logico-philosophicus*, 6.54 (trans. D. F. Pears and B. F. McGuinness). Wittgenstein is reputed to have written his famous *Tractatus* in the trenches as an Austrian soldier during the First World War. He sent his manuscript to Bertrand Russell, whom he already knew from an earlier period of study in England, and who immediately recognized its interest and importance.

   The sentence quoted indicates that, having seen his way in philosophy, as Wittgenstein then believed, he had no further use for it. Consistently with this, Wittgenstein worked in other occupations for the next twenty years, returning to philosophy only when he became dissatisfied with his earlier answers. There are thus an 'earlier' and a 'later' Wittgenstein, who approach philosophy in very different ways but who have both been enormously influential.

7. Epictetus, *Arrian's Discourses of Epictetus*, Book III, xxiv, 8-12. Passage specially translated for this volume by Christopher Strachan, University of Hull.

8. For an account of ancient Stoicism, see R. D. Hicks, *Stoic and Epicurean*; and for some readings in these philosophers, see J. L. Saunders (ed.), *Greek and Roman Philosophy after Aristotle*. The modern work referred to is *A Stoic Philosophy of Life* by Keith Campbell.

9. Epictetus, *Fragments*, 20 Stobaeus, III, 4.94 (Loeb, Vol. II, p. 465).

10. Spinoza, *The Principles of Descartes' Philosophy*.

11. Psalm 139, i-xiii; translation taken from New International Version of *The Holy Bible*.

12. Spinoza, *Ethics*, Part II, Prop. XI, Coroll.

13. ibid., Part III, Prop II, Note.

14. ibid., Part IV, Prop. LXVII.

Reading Guide to Chapter 7

Stoic and Epicurean by R. D. Hicks provides a readable account of these ancient systems; and there is a selection of readings in J. L. Saunders (ed.), *Greek and Roman Philosophy after Aristotle*. The argument from design as developed by the Stoics is presented by Cicero in *On the Nature of the Gods*.

Spinoza's *Ethics*, originally published in Latin in 1677 shortly after his death, is best read in a modern translation. In particular, see that by E. M. Curley.

For a readable and clear account of Spinoza, see S. Hampshire, *Spinoza*, or see the chapter on Spinoza in R. Scruton's *A Short History of Modern Philosophy*. This also includes chapters on other metaphysical systems: those of Descartes, Leibniz, Kant and Hegel. The contemporary philosopher T. L. S. Sprigge (b. 1932) defends a modern Spinozist point of view in *The Vindication of Absolute Idealism* and, more briefly, in Ch. 8 of his *Theories of Existence*.

8 Moving on

Two things fill the mind with ever new and increasing admiration and awe, the oftener and the more steadily we reflect on them: the starry heavens above and the moral law within.

– Immanuel Kant, *Critique of Practical Reason*

The glimpse I have just had of Spinoza's system had shown me the connection between two of the great dualisms of philosophy: the dualism of mind and matter – the mental and the physical – on the one hand, and the contrast between free will and determinism on the other.

The free will issue connects with my first concerns – what to do – what *we* as members of communities and citizens of the world should do – because some kind of 'mental' or spiritual freedom seems to be a condition of morality. This might not be so if I had accepted the possibility of translating the moral into other terms – for example, practical utility, local custom or biological drives – but I recall that my reflections left me with an intact notion of irreducible good and evil, right and wrong, and for this I need, in some way or other, to see myself as free to choose.

But this suggests another dichotomy – another dominating contrast – which underlies both the moral questions and the questions which, in philosophical terms, might be called ontological, linguistic and epistemological – questions, that is, about what there really *is*; about how I may talk about it; and how I may know it. *This* dichotomy can be described as the contrast between objectivity and subjectivity . . . between realism and anti-realism . . . between belief in some external ground of knowledge – some fact of the matter – and relativism.

I may think of this contrast first in relation to morality: does value belong to actions or situations lying outside myself in the world of other people, their doings and circumstances? Or is the attribution of value strictly a response of mine to the way things strike me?

This problem of objectivity is also, however, a problem about the world of science and the senses. It can be presented in terms of a story. Suppose, in some science-fiction world, a scientist had been able to remove my brain and place it in a vat of fluid; suppose it could be kept alive and computer-programmed to have all the experiences I now have. (This hypothesis does no more, of course, than place me in the same position as Descartes deceived by his 'malignant demon' – the hypothesis I encountered in Chapter 1 – but is has a more convincing science-fiction 'feel' about it.) Suppose furthermore that all memory of a previous life had been technolog-ically eliminated, would there be any way that I could distinguish my brain-in-a-vat existence from 'normal' human existence?

Already in my opening reflections I encountered problems of knowledge and of truth that are sharpened and pointed up by entertaining such fanciful sceptical hypotheses. There, too, I was obliged to consider questions of objectivity and subjectivity in relation to morals or principles for social living. Subsequently, I saw a similar debate opening up again in relation to science, this time as the contrast between rationalism and irrationalism. And then, later, thinking about language revealed to me important questions about reference and representation which I can now see also involved this problem of objectivity – a problem which is itself at bottom *the* problem of truth and knowledge of truth.

I have just used the world 'realism' to describe what I might see as a commitment to truth in the sense of a belief that there is some kind of correspondence between true assertions and the way the world is – a belief that there is, in other words, a fact of the matter. Accepting this, as I have so far done at each stage of my quest, provides one half of an answer to many of my initial questions as well as to others that I have encountered subsequently – an approach to an answer which involves the repudiation of scepticism, irrationalism and subjectivism. There is another half to my answer, though, that explains some of the recurring dichotomies my quest has exposed, and explains, too, why realism is not, after all, a terminus to philosophical discussion. This is that, nevertheless, my perceptions of that reality, that world, are conditioned by my own experience.

Bishop Berkeley, the eighteenth-century British philosopher, understood this well, pointing out that if we even *try* to imagine something unperceived-by-us, the very act of imagining places us in the picture, whether we like it or not. We can imagine only in terms of our own ways of perceiving. As the contemporary American philosopher, Hilary Putnam, has put this: 'There is a real world *but* we can only describe it in terms of our own conceptual system.'[1] The 'God's-eye' view, then, which the notion of objectivity might suggest, is not available to me. My perspective must be affected by the fact that it is *my* perspective.

I can now see that these problems of realism, reference, language and knowledge are inseparably linked together. I can see, also, that they may involve questions of value or morality, if that is sufficiently widely construed, since choosing a position here – deciding what rationality *is* – itself involves evaluation. It is in effect a moral stance. Since this is Putnam's view, too, I note that Putnam's own realist intuitions are set within a theory which he describes as a 'demythologized Kantianism'.

From Kant, Putnam believes, we can draw the lesson that 'everything we say about an object is of the form: it is such as to affect *us* in such-and-such a way. *Nothing at all* we say about any object describes the object as it is "in itself".'[2] Kant distinguished *noumena* (things as they really are) from *phenomena* (things as they appear to us), and pointed out that we are cut off from access to the former, confined to access to the latter. Putnam's 'mind-independent reality' is Kant's noumena or 'things-in-themselves'. But for Putnam, the noumenal world is simply what a rational being with our sense organs would construct – the way in which, not arbitrarily but inevitably, creatures like us *must* interpret our surroundings.

Putnam's neo-Kantianism, then, is essentially the view that at one level, within the empirical realm, truth can be viewed as correspondence with the facts, but that, nevertheless, at another level all truth is in the end mind-dependent. Putnam's appeal to Kant is direct: 'It is not that the thinking mind *makes up* the world in Kant's view;

but it doesn't just mirror it either'[3] or, more epigrammatically, 'the mind and the world jointly make up the mind and the world'.[4]

This is not, though, another restatement of relativism – of the view, that is, that truth is simply a matter of one's point of view. *That*, Putnam believes, is ultimately self-refuting. Relativism is essentially incoherent in that it is inconsistent both to *hold* a point of view and at the same time argue that *no* point of view is more justified or right than any other. It is self-defeating, too, in making it impossible to maintain a distinction between *being* right and *thinking* one is right – for no argument can be conducted on that basis.

Against this, the case for some kind of realism – for a claim that there *is* a fact of the matter – is strong. The strength of realism consists initially in the practical success of realist assumptions, even if later these may need some qualification, whether this is success in the field of science or success in terms of common-sense communication about material objects.

But a more sophisticated view of science and the physical world may lay stress on the way even the meaning of the words science uses to describe the world may change. And in the case of Kuhn and Feyerabend, for example, as I have already seen, this observation may be seen as anti-realist in its implications. To defend a realist perspective, then, it is necessary to deny this total fluidity of language and concepts and insist that change takes place only within certain parameters. Putnam, then, in maintaining a qualified realism, insists that there must be *some* convergence or constancy of meaning in scientific concepts, and that although our understanding of things may change, the scope for change is not totally unlimited. So, for example, 'electron' can't mean something now that has *nothing at all* in common with what it meant in the 1900s. It must either still refer to the same thing, or at least retain some of the same meaning – it must have either a shared reference, or a shared sense, in order to provide some kind of anchor-point for understanding, outside ourselves and our own thinking.

Finally, against relativist claims that what is accepted as true changes in step with changing human needs and interests, it is nevertheless possible to point to important factors in common between human beings, some universal aspects of human nature, which survive the test of time and which help to guarantee what

Putnam calls the 'universal intercommunicability of human cultures'. As he says, 'human *Interests*, human *saliencies*, human cognitive processes, must have a *structure* which is heavily determined by innate or constitutional factors. Human nature isn't all *that* plastic.'[5]

But this is not orthodox realism. It takes account of the reciprocity of internal and external factors, the dialectic between mind and the world. Putnam's aim is to break the traditional dichotomy – to find a middle ground between objectivism and relativism, to see the strength of the anti-realist case, but not to lose all purchase on the notion of reality. Indeed, he is prepared to sum up the entire programme for analytic philosophy in the twentieth century as 'the problem of how words "hook on to" the world'.[6]

The commitment to truth

At this point, I may now be in a position to look back and see some of the debates I have encountered as ways of dealing with that particular question, and also as providing some insight into the kind of problems that provided the starting point (in Chapter 1) for my quest. I started there with an initial commitment to two things only: truth and virtue. How, I may now ask, has that double commitment survived my inquiry? What, first, of the notion of truth?

Descartes, I can now see, set the problem for subsequent generations; although, as I have noted, the terms of the argument had already been sketched out in ancient times. He might not have recognized the problem under Putnam's brief idiomatic description – the problem of how words 'hook on to' the world – although he would surely have been in sympathy with the elegant economy and understandability of the phrase. After all, it was Descartes who initiated the modern breakthrough from esoteric language confined to the learned, to the ideal of describing philosophical problems in everyday language, and in terms that the ordinary person can understand.

The problem, then, concerns the gulf between what there is to know and our knowledge of it. That gulf exists when I think of ordinary everyday statements of observation; when I think of truths of logic or arithmetic; when I reason scientifically about what lies beyond my present experience; and even more when I consider moral, religious or aesthetic truth. It strikes me acutely when I consider the grounds on which I claim knowledge of the past or of other people's feelings; of the feelings, too, of animals; and even when I reflect on my knowledge of myself as a continuing being. In the past, the different ways of answering these questions might seem to have been summed up in the contrast between finding the answer through the exercise simply of reason itself – Descartes' own solution – or, as empiricist philosophers from Bacon onwards favoured, seeking for the primitive sense-observations which would provide the rock-bottom data from which to construct the edifice of knowledge.

In the first case, reason might provide an answer, as it did for Spinoza, in terms of a whole system of thought, in which it is impossible to answer a question about one aspect without, at least implicitly, describing the whole. In the second case, arriving at truth is a piecemeal process of observation and consolidation. Surprisingly, since I might have supposed that by now some agreement would have been reached on these issues, it is at a crossroads like this that I find philosophy at the present time – though now with scepticism on the part of some philosophers as to even the validity of the question.

The view that it is reason rather than observation that provides an integrated answer, an interlocking system of truth, is the essential characteristic of a metaphysical system. I know that much of this century's philosophy has been a reaction *against* metaphysics. Indeed, it was from the hegemony of such metaphysical systems as those of F. H. Bradley (1856–1924) and J. McTaggart (1866–1925) that G. E. Moore (1873–1958) and Bertrand Russell broke free at the turn of the century. As Russell described this in his intellectual autobiography:

> He [G. E. Moore] took the lead in rebellion, and I followed, with a sense of emancipation. Bradley argued that everything common sense believes in is mere appearance; we reverted to the opposite extreme, and thought that *everything* is real that common sense, uninfluenced by philosophy or theology, supposes real. With a sense of escaping from prison, we allowed ourselves to think that the grass is green, that the sun and stars would exist if no one was aware of them, and also that there is a pluralistic timeless

world of Platonic ideas. The world, which had been thin and logical, suddenly became rich and varied and solid.[7]

Moore and Russell, I know, were both unable to hold to this simple perception of our knowledge of the world, but the attempt was symbolic of the twentieth-century preoccupations of philosophy: philosophy under the dominance of science. 'Scientism' consists, essentially, of the view that there are appropriate criteria for the solution of well-defined problems and that rationality is a matter of applying them. It epitomized the desire for objectivity. Its quintessential expression was the logical positivism of the 1930s, which was dominated by the two dogmas of (a) the analytic/synthetic distinction and (b) the idea that empirical knowledge is constructed from simple, incontrovertible foundations. Its basic assumption is that there is just one truth. This is the notion of convergence, of the possibility of a consensus of all reasonable – or all rational – people.

But I have seen how this notion of convergence, and hence of the inter-translatability of systems of thought and ideas – of different 'languages' or conceptual systems – is under challenge today. The attack on the idea of convergence, the metaphor of inquiry, the belief in the possibility of a unified science and a common conception of truth is well summed up in the American philosopher Richard Rorty's dismissal of such aims as old-fashioned religion – the kind of 'motives which once led us to posit gods'.[8] It displays a tendency, Rorty believes, to claim a broad human perspective for what is in reality no more than a 'lonely provincialism'. We should see ourselves, therefore – and 'we' are 'the liberal Rawlsian searchers for consensus, the heirs of Socrates, the people who wish to link their days dialectically each to each'[9] – as representing just one of many possible movements in human society, not as typifying a tradition open to, and common to, all human beings by virtue simply of their reason and common humanity.

But it was Quine who first opened the Pandora's box which dealt the death-blow to the 'scientistic' assumptions of analytic philosophy. Although himself a representative of the analytic tradition, Quine has supplied a holistic turn which has led to a new favouring of coherence over correspondence in theories about what truth consists in – a turn which fits well with the pragmatist traditions of

American philosophy. Holism is the view that partial truths cannot stand alone – every partial truth implies the whole of which it is part. But Quine's holism is not sceptical – it consists in the idea that science is essentially a two-tier network of sentences: a central core of sentences which are only with reluctance relinquished, and other, peripheral ones which can more readily be revised in the light of experience. In Quine's view, it is a network of sentences like these that, when adopted by a particular community, constitutes a conceptual scheme.

Davidson's challenge to the 'very idea of conceptual scheme' is therefore yet more radical and iconoclastic in its implications. For in suggesting that it is impossible to conceive of *alternative* conceptual schemes, Davidson is saying that the idea of a conceptual scheme is in itself incoherent. He attacks the 'dogma of the dualism of scheme and reality', claiming that concepts do not depend on an uninterpreted reality. It is believing in this *dualism* – believing that there are two things: a conceptual scheme *and* reality – that leads, in his view, to conceptual relativism, and to the notion that *truth* is relative to a conceptual scheme. He says: 'In giving up the dualism of scheme and world, we do not give up the world, but re-establish unmediated touch with the familiar objects whose antics make our sentences and opinions true or false.'[10]

Davidson's holism is therefore of a different order from Quine's. Nevertheless, both are agreed in taking the step that is the distinctive hallmark of holism: this is to say that the basic units of significance are not isolated sentences but rather whole systems of sentences. Truth can therefore be a quality only of the whole, not of any individual element. This, which was the distinguishing characteristic of the great metaphysical systems constructed on rationalist foundations, is essentially the standpoint I now find in common between those contemporary heirs to the analytic tradition, Quine, Davidson and, indeed, Putnam too, in spite of his realist aspirations.

But this means that the question of truth can no longer be seen, as the positivists saw it, in terms of the analytic/synthetic distinction. In place of that distinction, which carefully separated truths of meaning (analytic truths) to be arrived at by reflective reasoning from truths of substance (synthetic truths), there is a new unified approach, a 'methodological monism' which rejects the empiricist's clear line of demarcation. And since different or alternative 'true' pictures of the world become possible on this understanding of things, the move from correspondence to coherence as a test for truth is also a step in the direction of pragmatism – usually understood as the theory that a statement is true if believing that it is so works in practice. From such a perspective, which is indeed that of Rorty, the belief that observations are theory-laden leads to the view that ideas, words and language are not mirrors which copy the 'real' or 'objective' world, but rather tools people use to cope with their environment.

As I have seen, Putnam is willing to concede this to some extent. He says: 'The idea that truth is a passive copy of what is "really" (mind-independently, discourse-independently) "there" has collapsed under the critiques of Kant, Wittgenstein and other philosophers even if it continues to have a deep hold on our thinking.'[11]

So Putnam agrees with these philosophers in rejecting the idea that there is just one true and complete description of the way the world is – he calls this the 'externalist' or 'God's-eye' view. Indeed, his answer to the brains-in-a-vat problem is that it can be rejected simply because there *is* no God's-eye view from which to tell the story. As he puts it: 'If we are Brains in a Vat, we cannot think that we are.' It follows, then, that it is not *possible* that we are.[12]

Nevertheless, words cannot *simply* be tools to cope with our environment – both the notion of 'ourselves' and the notion of 'environment' smuggle back the realist conceptions that are being attacked in such arguments.

But Putnam, unlike Rorty, seeks to retain the essence of realism. He does this through the notion of rational acceptability: the criterion for a fact, he suggests, is what it is rational to accept. This is a concept of rationality not restricted to science. To assume that restriction would be yet another hangover from positivism. Many current views of truth, Putnam claims, are alienated views: 'They cause one to lose one part of one's self and the world, to see the world as simply consisting of elementary particles swerving in the void (the "physicalist" view . . .) or to see the world as simply consisting of "actual and possible sense-data" (the older empiricist view), or to deny that there is a world at all.'[13]

In place of the 'God's-eye' view, then, Putnam puts what he calls an 'internalist' perspective. By this he means, to begin with, that the question 'What objects does the world consist of?' admits of more than one true answer. It also means that the question itself can only be asked *within* a theory or description. Putnam insists that truth is 'ideal coherence of our beliefs with each other and with our experi- ence *as these experiences are themselves represented in our belief system*'. [14] It is this that Putnam means by the notion of rational acceptability, and, unlike the straightforwardly objective notion of truth, it is not fixed by some immutable book of rules. It is a flexible notion: what it is rational to accept depends on who you are and where you are.

However, Putnam does not see this as a break with objectivity. On the contrary, it provides, he believes, as much as we can aspire to: that is, 'objectivity for us'. To achieve this it may be necessary to follow a Kantian procedure of transcendental investigation – the kind of investigation, that is, that explores the 'preconditions of reference and hence of thought – preconditions built into the nature of our minds themselves'.[15]

So Putnam's 'internalism' is not a facile relativism that says, 'Any- thing goes.' As he says, I *could* adopt a conceptual scheme in which I could fly, but I would soon find something wrong with that scheme if I tried to jump out of the window. Internal coherence, in other words, is not the *only* constraint on what I may think. The rules are not immutable, but it would be irrational to try to construct and reconstruct them according to the arbitrary whim of the moment. Our notions of coherence and acceptability are 'deeply interwoven with our psychology. They depend upon our biology and our cul- ture', and 'Objectivity and rationality humanly speaking are what we have; they are better than nothing.'[16]

Our experience is limited, however, and our biology fallible. This is what sets limits to our ability to build up an unchallengeable picture of the world. So 'We use our criteria of rational acceptability to build up a theoretical picture of the "empirical world" and then as that picture develops we revise our very criteria of rational acceptability in the light of that picture and so on and so on forever.'[17]

The commitment to virtue

So Putnam's 'objectivity for us' is not a final destination, even if it is a claim to a more substantial reality than some overtly relativistic and irrationalist alternatives. It connects, too, with the second commitment which I acknowledged at the beginning of my inquiry: the commitment to virtue.

The connection is a double one. First, what it is rational for me to believe is essentially connected with the sort of creature that I am. So a theory of human nature is presupposed in the answers I give to these deep epistemological questions. And the question of what human nature is is in itself an issue which is partly empirical, partly evaluative. Biology, history, psychology, sociology all contribute to a view of human nature. But so, too, does our judgement of what is ideal, as opposed to what merely happens to be the case. Social arrangements, economics, the interference or malevolence of other people, may all contribute to making what human nature currently *is* different from what ideally it might be.

But secondly, both Putnam and Rorty, different though their views may be, come close to accepting something like the American pragmatist William James's (1842–1909) view of truth as 'the name for whatever proves itself to be good in the way of belief'.[18]

This linking of truth and goodness at the heart of a philosophical theory shatters the remaining dichotomy to which philosophy has clung in its positivistic phase – the gulf Hume claimed to detect between facts and values.[19] This explains why 'objectivity for us' is, as a matter of fact, a concept which is as applicable in the realm of values as it is in the realm of facts. My conclusions (in Chapter 3) about the need for a common world order committed to basic human rights; my observations (in Chapter 2) about a range of positive values common to human beings for personal and domestic living; these are aspirations connected, as is Putnam's notion of rationality, with some notion of human flourishing.

'Objectivity for us' in the realm of morals involves renouncing the claim that values are 'out there' to be discovered – that there is a 'God's-eye' view. But it also involves renouncing the suggestion that in morals and politics 'anything goes'. Again, by careful garnering of the facts about human beings, by drawing a picture of human nature as it is, but also by using this factual information to form a conception of what it might be, it is possible to answer some of the questions about values, too, with which I began my quest.

On the very widest front, I can see how a total conception of such a moral ideal would involve an awareness of human beings within the context of their physical (geographical, biological and social) existence. Hence the widest political and moral values must be dictated by environmental concern. Learning to live in harmony with nature may be the first priority for securing a setting within which human nature itself can flourish.

But if I take 'environment' to mean more than fresh air, living forests, clean lakes and an unbroken chain of animal life; if I interpret it positively as 'making the place that we are good', then that apparently apolitical environmentalist goal becomes immediately political in a narrower sense. For the 'setting' within which human beings may hope to flourish must include the way people treat each other, as well as the way they treat the planet.

Again I am confronted with large questions, and large strategies seem to be dictated to me by my reflections on both facts and values. I can see the point of Plato's parable of the shackled prisoners in the cave (described in Chapter 7). There is a time for reflection on the widest and most abstract of truths – indeed, on the question of truth itself – and this is the traditional concern of philosophy. But there is a pressing need for action, as well as for philosophical reflection. Even the limited aim of creating a world that makes possible the practice of philosophy – an activity for which both leisure and freedom are essential – is a challenge of enormous dimensions. Perhaps this is why Kant so emphatically linked contemplation of the physical world – the 'starry heavens above' – to attention to 'the moral law within'. Perhaps, too, it is the reason why Russell, writing in the twentieth century, found his own contemplation of philosophy deflected earthwards by the 'echoes of cries of pain' that tore him from his private pursuit of love and knowledge.

For me, no less than these, philosophical reflection must give place to action, or at least to a programme of commitment to the values I would wish to see embodied in social and personal living. Perhaps this can only express itself in a negative way: that I will not add to the pain which I detect around me; that if I cannot build, then at least I will not destroy. And in so far as pain and death are unavoidable aspects of human existence, perhaps I will try to cultivate that acceptance of the whole of which these are parts recommended by Spinoza and the Stoics.

Last thoughts

My initial commitment, then, was to truth and virtue. I have followed this commitment through, and find that it has, in effect, brought me full circle. I passed from personal decision-making to social and political action, finally touching on the most abstract and detached questions of language, logic, realism and representation. From there I found myself faced with the task of forming a conception of human nature, which itself in turn now compels me to form a view of the kind of social and political setting within which human nature can reach its ideal fulfilment.

But as an individual, there may be little I can do to affect these grand questions of global strategy. It may be that I will be obliged to retreat closer to what most directly concerns me: those intimate domestic and workplace situations where indeed I can make a difference to the potential of others for 'flourishing' – for their personal happiness and fulfilment.

Even here, though, my power to affect others must be limited. So that, in the end, I may find that it is only my own moral character that is ultimately within my control. And here it is the notion of personal integrity, of choosing the kind of life I would like to have led, the kind of person I would like to have been, that will be the ultimate test of the validity of both my inquiry and my conclusions.

But this is far from being a counsel of despair. As Putnam says: 'If we are doomed to have neither a computer's-eye view nor a God's-eye view of ourselves and each other, is that such a terrible fate? We are men and women; and men and women we may be lucky enough to remain. Let us try to preserve our humanity by, among other things, taking a humane view of ourselves and our self-knowledge.'[20]

Perhaps, though, I still have some hankerings after those grand notions of God, immortality and the soul which I hoped philosophy might supply for me. If so, I may reflect on some words written to me a long time ago by Sophia:

You didn't think, because there is nothing separate that was mind, there is no mind. So you should not think that, if there is nothing separate which is God, there is no God; or if nothing separate which is soul, that there is no soul. It is not absurd, or ultimately incomprehensible, to say that the world is God, mind, soul; that this is the only path to immortality; and that understanding this is the only peace of mind.

Some people turn to the East for this sort of insight – Buddhist and Hindu religion is not antipathetic to these ideas; fatalism and integration with nature are two common strands in those systems of belief. But you chose me as your guru, and I represent a more austere, but enormously fruitful, tradition. You will have to be mentally and emotionally stronger to take your sustenance from me. But Western religious traditions are strong, too, and nothing I have said is incompatible with an open and compassionate religious faith. After all, in ethical stance, Socrates and Jesus have striking elements in common with each other and against the traditions of careless, evil or unthinking people.

But create for yourself your own notion of deity or of God, and then look for it in the people and the traditions you find around you. Do not neglect nature, either, as a source of useful instruction, and do not ignore the lessons of birth and death, termination and renewal that nature silently teaches.

And if you can share with others what you know, or the values that this compels you to hold, then this knowledge and these values can themselves become part of the common mind – the common store of wisdom – which has the power to outlast the individual. For that, really, is what philosophy is: not an esoteric discipline, but the common endeavour of the human race to understand and come to terms with its own perilous, fragile and ultimately ephemeral existence.

Notes to Chapter 8

1. H. Putnam, *Meaning and the Moral Sciences*, p. 32.
2. H. Putnam, *Reason, Truth and History*, pp. 60–61.
3. H. Putnam, *Meaning and the Moral Sciences*, p. 1.

4. H. Putnam, *Reason, Truth and History*, p. xi.

5. H. Putnam, *Meaning and the Moral Sciences*, p. 56.

6. H. Putnam, 'After Empiricism', in *Post-analytic Philosophy*, ed. J. Rajchman and C. West.

7. B. Russell, 'My mental development', in P. A. Schilpp (ed.), p. 12.

8. R. Rorty, 'Solidarity or Objectivity?', in J. Rajchman and C. West, op. cit., p. 10.

9. ibid., p. 12.

10. D. Davidson, 'On the Very Idea of a Conceptual Scheme', D. Davidson, *Enquiries into Truth and Interpretation*, p. 198.

11. H. Putnam, *Reason, Truth and History*, p. 128.

12. ibid., pp. xi–xii.

13. ibid., pp. 50–51.

14. ibid., p. 50.

15. ibid., p. 16.

16. ibid., p. 55.

17. ibid., p. 184.

18. W. James, *Pragmatism*, p. 42.

19. In a famous passage in his *Treatise of Human Nature*, III, 1, 1, first published 1739–40, Hume drew attention to the problem of passing from reasoning about what *is* to what *ought* to be. For an account of Hume's argument in its historical setting, see A. MacIntyre, *A Short History of Ethics*, Ch. 12.

20. H. Putnam, *Meaning and the Moral Sciences*, p. 77.

Reading Guide to Chapter 8

John Passmore's *Recent Philosophers* provides an excellent guide to the most recent preoccupations of philosophers. See in particular Ch. 5, 'Realism and Relativism', for discussion of some of the topics touched on in this chapter, and for an account of their context and relationship to other aspects of contemporary philosophy not touched on here. Passmore's book includes, on these issues and others mentioned in this volume, detailed and descriptive guides to further reading of an advanced nature in current academic philosophy.

Putnam's own work is best approached through *Reason, Truth and History* and *Meaning and the Moral Sciences*. There is also a three-volume collection of his papers, of which the second, *Mind, Language and Reality*, is of most relevance to issues discussed earlier in this book, while Volume 3, *Realism and Reason*, is particularly concerned with the issue of realism.

Richard Rorty's views are to be found in his *Philosophy and the Mirror of Nature* and *Consequences of Pragmatism*. H. Morick's (ed.) *Challenges to Empiricism* provides an important collection of critical essays exploring new directions. Authors include Quine, Carnap, Popper, Feyerabend and

Chomsky. For a further example of a Kantian revival, see W. Sellars, *Science and Metaphysics*.

A variety of views on what philosophy is by well-known philosophers, including, among others, J. J. C. Smart, Karl Popper, Brand Blanshard and Sidney Hook, may be found in *The Owl of Minerva*, eds. C. J. Bontempo and S. J. Odell.

Appendix: The Kant Mottoes

The quotations from Kant at the beginning of each chapter are from the following sources:

Chapter 1: See T. K. Abbott, 'Memoir of Kant', in Kant's *Critique of Practical Reason and other works on the theory of ethics*, trans. T. K. Abbott, London: Longmans (1st Edn 1879) 6th edn 1909, photoreprinted, 1954, p. xxxiii.

Chapter 2: *Immanuel Kant's Critique of Pure Reason*, trans. N. K. Smith, London: Macmillan, 1963, A 805; B 833; NKS 635.

Chapter 3: *Perpetual Peace*, AA 380 in *Kant's Political Writings*. Edited with an introduction and notes by Hans Reiss, trans. H. B. Nisbet, Cambridge: Cambridge University Press, 1970.

Chapter 4: *Immanuel Kant's Critique of Pure Reason*, trans. N. K. Smith, London: Macmillan, 1963, A 305; B 362; NKS 305.

Chapter 5: *Immanuel Kant's Critique of Pure Reason*, trans. N. K. Smith, London: Macmillan, 1963, A 51; B 75; NKS 93.

Chapter 6: *The Moral Law. Kant's Groundwork of the Metaphysic of Morals*, trans. H. Paton, London: Hutchinson (1st edn 1948), AA 448.

Chapter 7: Immanuel Kant, *Prolegomena*, trans. P. Lucas, Manchester: Manchester University Press, 1953, AA 274 PL 28.

Chapter 8: *Kant's Critique of Practical Reason and other works on the theory of ethics*, trans. T. K. Abbott, London: Longmans, p. 260.

Bibliography

Chapter 1

Augustine, *Confessions*, trans. R. S. Pine-Coffin, Harmondsworth: Penguin, 1961

Ayer, A. J., *The Problem of Knowledge*, Harmondsworth: Penguin, 1976
  Foundations of Empirical Knowledge, London: Macmillan, 1975
  The Central Questions of Philosophy, Harmondsworth: Penguin, 1976

Copleston, F. C., *A History of Philosophy*, rev. edn, New York: Doubleday 'Image Books', 1962–6; 3–vol. edn, 1985

Davies, N., *God's Playground*, Oxford: Clarendon, 1981

Descartes, R., *Meditations*, in *The Philosophical Writings of Descartes*, Vol. 2, trans. J. Cottingham, R. Stoothoff, and D. Murdoch, Cambridge: Cambridge University Press, 1985

Hollis, M., *An Invitation to Philosophy*, Oxford: Blackwell, 1985

Magee, B. (ed.), *Men of Ideas*, Oxford: Oxford University Press, 1982

Montefiore, A., Review of H. G. Skilling's 'Charter 77 and Human Rights in Czechoslovakia', *Journal of Applied Philosophy* 1, 1984

O'Connor, D. J. (ed.), *A Critical History of Western Philosophy*, Glencoe: Free Press, 1964

O'Hear, A., *What Philosophy Is*, Harmondsworth: Penguin, 1985

Passmore, J., *A Hundred Years of Philosophy*, Harmondsworth: Penguin, 1968
  Recent Philosophers: a supplement to A Hundred Years of Philosophy, London: Duckworth, 1985

Plato, *The Last Days of Socrates*, trans. H. Tredennick, Harmondsworth: Penguin, 1968. Contains *Euthyphro, Apology, Crito, Phaedo*. Also available in *Dialogues of Plato*, Vol. 1, trans. B. Jowett, London: Sphere, 1970; or in *The Collected Dialogues*, ed. E. Hamilton and H. Cairns, Princeton, New Jersey: Princeton University Press, 1961

Russell, B., *The Problems of Philosophy*, London: Oxford University Press, 1986. First published 1912
  A History of Western Philosophy, London: Allen & Unwin, 1984

Scruton, R., *A Short History of Modern Philosophy*, London: Routledge & Kegan Paul, 1984

Skilling, H. G., *Charter 77 and Human Rights in Czechoslovakia*, London: Allen & Unwin, 1981

Smart, J. J. C., *Problems of Space and Time*, New York: Macmillan, 1964

Vesey, G. (ed.), *Philosophy in the Open*, Milton Keynes: Open University Press, 1974

Williams, B., *Problems of the Self*, Cambridge: Cambridge University Press, 1973

Wittgenstein, L., *Philosophical Investigations*, 3rd edn, trans. G. E. M. Anscombe, Oxford: Blackwell, 1968

Chapter 2

Almond, B., *Moral Concerns*, Englewood Cliffs, New Jersey: The Humanities Press, 1987

Anscombe, E., 'Modern Moral Philosophy', in *Collected Philosophical Papers, Vol. 3, Ethics, Religion and Politics*, Oxford: Blackwell, 1981

Aristotle, *Nichomachean Ethics*, rev. edn, trans. H. Tredennick, Harmondsworth: Penguin, 1976; or see *Nichomachean Ethics*, trans. M. Ostwald, Indianapolis: Bobbs-Merrill, 1962

Bentham, J., *An Introduction to the Principles of Morals and Legislation*, London: Athlone Press, 1970

Bok, S., *Lying*, New York: Random House, 1979
  Secrets, New York: Random House, 1984

Butler, J., *Fifteen Sermons*, in *The Works of Joseph Butler*, ed. W. E. Gladstone, Oxford: Clarendon Press, 1896. Also published in *Butler's Fifteen Sermons* ed. T. A. Roberts, London: S.P.C.K., 1970

Epictetus, *Moral Discourses*, trans. W. A. Oldfather, London: Heinemann, 1925 (Vol. 1), 1928 (Vol. 2); or trans. Carter, London: Dent, 1910

Ezorsky, G. (ed.), *Moral Rights in the Workplace*, New York: S.U.N.Y. Press, 1986

Foot, P. (ed.), *Theories of Ethics*, London: Oxford University Press, 1967

Frankena, W., *Ethics*, 2nd edn, Englewood Cliffs, New Jersey: Prentice-Hall, 1973

Gilligan, C., 'In a Different Voice: Women's Conceptions of Self and Morality', *Harvard Educational Review* 47, 1977. Also in a later version as Ch. 3 of *In a Different Voice*, Cambridge, Mass.: Harvard University Press, 1982

Glover, J., *Causing Death and Saving Lives*, Harmondsworth: Penguin, 1977

Hare, R. M., 'Principles', *Proc. of the Aristotelian Society* 73, 1972–3
  Freedom and Reason, London: Oxford University Press, 1963
  Moral Thinking, London: Oxford University Press, 1981

Hume, D., *Enquiries Concerning Human Understanding and Concerning the Principles of Morals*, ed. L. A. Selby-Bigge, rev. edn P. Nidditch, London: Oxford University Press 1975, reprinted from 1777 edition.

Hursthouse, R., *Beginning Lives*, Oxford: Blackwell, 1988

Kant, I., *Groundwork of the Metaphysics of Morals* as *The Moral Law*, ed. H. Paton, London: Hutchinson, 1948

MacIntyre, A., *A Short History of Ethics*, London: Routledge & Kegan Paul, 1967

Mackie, J., *Ethics*, Harmondsworth: Penguin, 1977

  'Can there be a right-based moral theory?' in Waldron, J. (ed.)

Melden, A. I., *Rights and Persons*, Oxford: Blackwell, 1977

Midgley, M., *Wickedness*, London: Routledge & Kegan Paul, 1984

Mill, J. S., *Utilitarianism*, London: Dent, 1954

Plato, *The Collected Dialogues*, ed. E. Hamilton and H. Cairns, Princeton, New Jersey: Princeton University Press, 1961; or see separately: *The Republic*, 2nd edn, trans. D. Lee, Harmondsworth: Penguin, 1974

  The Last Days of Socrates, trans. H. Tredennick, Harmondsworth: Penguin, 1969

  Gorgias, trans. W. Hamilton, Harmondsworth: Penguin, 1960

  Protagoras and Meno, trans. W. K. C. Guthrie, Harmondsworth: Penguin, 1956

Rachels, J. (ed.), *Moral Problems*, 3rd edn, New York: Harper & Row, 1979

Rawls, J., *A Theory of Justice*, Cambridge, Mass.: Harvard University Press, 1971

Reid, C. L. (ed.), *Choice and Action*, New York: Macmillan, 1981

Richards, J. R., *The Sceptical Feminist*, Harmondsworth: Penguin, 1982

Ryle, G., *Dilemmas*, Cambridge: Cambridge University Press, 1954

Smart, J. J. C., and B. Williams, *Utilitarianism: For and Against*, Cambridge: Cambridge University Press, 1973

Waldron, J. (ed.), *Theories of Rights*, Oxford: Oxford University Press, 1984

Wasserstrom, R. (ed.), *Today's Moral Problems*, 2nd edn, New York: Macmillan, 1979

Williams, B., *Ethics and the Limits of Philosophy*, London: Fontana, 1985

Chapter 3

Arblaster, A., *The Rise and Decline of Western Liberalism*, Oxford: Blackwell, 1984

Austin, J., *The Province of Jurisprudence Determined*, ed. H. L. A. Hart, London: Weidenfeld & Nicolson, 1954

Aristotle, *The Politics*, trans. T. A. Sinclair, rev. edn T. J. Saunders, Harmondsworth: Penguin, 1981.

Benn, S. I., 'Deterrence or Appeasement? or, On Trying to be Rational about Nuclear War', *Journal of Applied Philosophy*, I, 1984

Berlin, I., 'Two Concepts of Liberty', in *Four Essays on Liberty*, London: University Press, 1969

Devlin, P., *The Enforcement of Morals*, Oxford: Oxford University Press, 1978; or extract in R. Dworkin (ed.) *The Philosophy of Law*

Dworkin, R. M., *Taking Rights Seriously*, Cambridge, Mass.: Harvard University Press, 1977

  (ed.), *The Philosophy of Law*, Oxford: Oxford University Press, 1977

Elliot, R., and A. Gare (eds.), *Environmental Philosophy*, Milton Keynes: Open University Press, 1983

Glucksmann, A., *La Force du Vertige*, Paris: Grasset, 1983

Gramsci, A., *Prison Notebooks*, ed. Q. Hoare and P. Nowell-Smith, London: Lawrence & Wishart, 1973

Gray, J., *Liberalism*, Milton Keynes; Open University Press, 1986

Hampshire, S. (ed.), *Public and Private Morality*, Cambridge: Cambridge University Press, 1978

Hart, H. L. A., *Law, Liberty and Morality*, London: Oxford University Press, 1971

  The Concept of Law, London: Oxford University Press, 1976

Hayek, F. A., *The Road to Serfdom*, London: Routledge & Kegan Paul, 1976. First published 1944

Hobbes, T., *Leviathan*, ed. C. P. Macpherson, Harmondsworth: Penguin, 1981. First published 1651

Kamen, H. *The Rise of Toleration*, London: Weidenfeld & Nicolson, 1967

Kamenka, E. (ed.), *The Portable Karl Marx*, Harmondsworth: Penguin, 1983

Kelsen, H., *The Pure Theory of Law*, Berkeley and Los Angeles: University of California Press, 1967, trans. M. Knight

Locke, J., *Two Treatises of Government*, rev. edn, introduction and notes by P. Laslett, New York: Mentor, 1965. First published 1690

Mabbott, J. D., *The State and the Citizen*, 2nd edn, London: Hutchinson, 1956

Marx, K., *The Communist Manifesto*, Harmondsworth: Penguin, 1967. Also in *Marx and Engels: Basic Writings on Politics and Philosophy*, ed. L. S. Feuer, Fontana, 1969; or see D. McLellan (ed.) *Karl Marx: Selected Writings*, Oxford University Press, 1977

McCloskey, H. J., *Ecological Ethics and Politics*, New Jersey: Rowan & Littlefield, 1983

Meadows, D. H., *et al.*, *The Limits to Growth*, New York: Universe Books, 1972

Mill, J. S., *Three Essays*, ed. R. Wollheim, Oxford: Oxford University Press, 1975. Contains *On Liberty, Representative Government* and *On the Subjection of Women*; or see *On Liberty*, Harmondsworth: Penguin, 1982. Also in *Utilitarianism, Liberty, and Representative Government*, London: Dent, 1910 and subsequent reprints

Nozick, R., *Anarchy, State and Utopia*, Oxford: Blackwell, 1974

O'Neill, O., *Faces of Hunger*, London: Allen & Unwin, 1986

Osborne, R., and R. Edgley (eds.), *Radical Philosophy Reader*, London: Verso/New Left Books, 1985

Passmore, J., *Man and His Place in Nature: Ecological Problems and Western Traditions*, London: Duckworth, 1980

Pelczynski, J., and J. Gray (eds.), *Conceptions of Liberty in Political Philosophy*, London: Athlone Press, 1984

Philips, R., *War and Justice*, Norman: University of Oklahoma Press, 1984

Plato, *Republic*, 2nd edn, trans. D. Lee, Harmondsworth: Penguin, 1974. Also available in *Dialogues of Plato* Vol. 4, trans. B. Jowett, ed. R. M. Hare and D. A. Russell, London: Sphere, 1970; or in *The Collected Dialogues*, ed. E. Hamilton and H. Cairns, Princeton, New Jersey: Princeton University Press, 1961

Popper, K., *The Poverty of Historicism*, 2nd edn, London: Routledge & Kegan Paul, 1961

Quinton, A. (ed.), *Political Philosophy*, Oxford University Press, 1967

Rachels, J. (ed.), *Moral Problems*, 2nd edn, New York: Harper & Row, 1975

Rawls, J., *A Theory of Justice*, Cambridge, Mass.: Harvard University Press, 1971

Redhead, B. (ed.), *Political Thought from Plato to Nato*, London: BBC Publications, 1984

Rousseau, J. J., *The Social Contract and Discourses*, trans. G. D. H. Cole. Revised by J. J. Bromfit and J. C. Hall, London: Dent, 1973. Contains *Discourse on the Origins of Inequality* and *The Social Contract*; or *The Social Contract*, trans. M. Cranston, Harmondsworth: Penguin, 1968; and *Discourse on Inequality*, trans. M. Cranston, Harmondsworth: Penguin, 1984; or R. D. Masters (ed.), *On the Social Contract*, trans. J. R. Masters, New York: St Martin's Press, 1978

Sassoon, A., *Gramsci's Politics*, New York: St Martin, 1980

Singer, P., *Practical Ethics*, Cambridge: Cambridge University Press, 1979
  'Famine, Affluence and Morality', *Philosophy and Public Affairs*, 1, 1972, pp. 229–43

Waldron, J. (ed.), *Theories of Rights*, Oxford: Oxford University Press, 1984

Walzer, M., *Just and Unjust Wars*, Harmondsworth: Penguin, 1987. First published 1977

Wasserstrom, R. (ed.), *Today's Moral Problems*, 2nd edn, New York: Macmillan, 1979
  War and Morality, Belmont, California: Wadsworth, 1970

Chapter 4

Ackermann, R., *Modern Deductive Logic*, London: Macmillan, 1970

Anderson, A. R., and N. D. Belnap Jr, *Entailment*, Vol. 1, Princeton, New Jersey: Princeton University Press, 1975

Aristotle, *Organon*, trans. H. Cooke and H. Tredennick, London: Heinemann, 1938

Ayer, A. J., *Philosophy in the Twentieth Century*, London: Allen & Unwin, 1984
  Language, Truth and Logic, Harmondsworth: Penguin, 1971. First published 1936; 2nd rev. edn 1946

Ayer, A. J. *et al.*, *The Revolution in Philosophy*, London: Macmillan, 1956
  (ed.), *Logical Positivism*, London: Macmillan, 1959

Bradley, R., and N. Swartz, *Possible Worlds: an introduction to logic and its philosophy*, Oxford: Blackwell, 1979

Burnet, J., *Early Greek Philosophy*, 4th edn, London: A. & C. Black, 1945

Carnap, R., *The Logical Foundations of Probability*, 2nd edn, Chicago: University of Chicago Press, 1962

Chalmers, A. F., *What is This Thing Called Science?*, 2nd edn, Open University Press, 1982

Feyerabend, P. K., 'Against Method, a Defence of Anarchy', *Minnesota Studies in the Philosophy of Science*, IV, eds. M. Radner and S. Winoker, Minneapolis: University of Minnesota Press, 1970, pp. 17–130

 Against Method, London: New Left Books, 1975

Flew, A., *Thinking about Thinking*, Fontana, 1985

Gale, R. M. (ed.), *The Philosophy of Time*, London: Macmillan, 1968. Or in Atlantic Highlands, New Jersey: Humanities Press, 1978

Goodman, N., *Fact, Fiction and Forecast*, 4th edn, Cambridge, Mass.: Harvard University Press, 1978

Grünbaum, A., *Modern Science and Zeno's Paradoxes*, London: Allen & Unwin, 1968

Haack, S., *Deviant Logic*, Cambridge: Cambridge University Press, 1975

 Philosophy of Logics, Cambridge: Cambridge University Press, 1978

Hacking, I., *Representing and Intervening*, Cambridge: Cambridge University Press, 1983

 (ed.), *Scientific Revolutions*, London: Oxford University Press, 1982

Hanfling, O., *Logical Positivism*, Oxford: Blackwell, 1981

 (ed.), *Essential Readings in Logical Positivism*, Oxford: Blackwell, 1981

Hughes, G. E., and K. G. Cresswell, *An Introduction to Modal Logic*, London: Methuen, 1968

Hume, D., *Enquiries Concerning Human Understanding and Concerning the Principles of Morals*, ed. L. A. Selby-Bigge, rev. edn P. H. Nidditch, London: Oxford University Press, 1977

Jeffrey, R. C., *Formal Logic: Its Scope and Limits*, 2nd edn, New York: McGraw-Hill, 1981

Kant, I., *Critique of Pure Reason*, trans. N. K. Smith, London: Macmillan, 1963. First published 1791; 2nd edn 1787

Kuhn, T. S., *The Structure of Scientific Revolutions*, 2nd edn, Chicago: University of Chicago Press, 1970

Lakatos, I., and A. E. Musgrave (eds.), *Criticism and the Growth of Knowledge*, Cambridge: Cambridge University Press, 1970

Leibniz, G. W., *Monadology*, available in *Leibniz: Philosophical Writings* ed. G. H. R. Parkinson, London: Dent, 1973

Lemmon, E. J., *Beginning Logic*, London: Nelson, 1981

Lewis, D., *Counterfactuals*, Oxford: Blackwell, 1973

 On the Plurality of Worlds, Oxford: Blackwell, 1986

Linsky, L. (ed.), *Reference and Modality*, London: Oxford University Press, 1971

McClean, G. F., and P. J. Aspell (eds.), *Readings in Ancient Western Philosophy*, New York: Appleton-Century-Crofts, 1970

Mill, J. S., *A System of Logic*, London: Longmans, 1949

Newton-Smith, W., *The Rationality of Science*, London: Routledge & Kegan Paul, 1981

Plato, *The Collected Dialogues*, eds. E. Hamilton and H. Cairns, Princeton, New Jersey: Princeton University Press, 1961

Popper, K., *Conjectures and Refutations*, 3rd edn, London: Routledge & Kegan Paul, 1969

   Objective Knowledge, London: Oxford University Press, 1973

   The Logic of Scientific Discovery, London: Hutchinson, 1974

Quine, W. V., *Methods of Logic*, 4th edn, Cambridge, Mass.: Harvard University Press, 1982

   From a Logical Point of View, New York: Harper & Row, 1953; 2nd rev. edn 1961, 63

   Philosophy of Logic, Englewood Cliffs, New Jersey: Prentice-Hall, 1970

   Selected Logic Papers, New York: Random House, 1966

Rist, J. M., *The Stoics*, Berkeley: University of California Press, 1978

Routley, R., and V. Routley, 'Rehabilitating Meinong's Theory of Objects', *Revue internationale de philosophie* 27, 1973

Routley, R. et al., *Relevant Logics and their Rivals*, Atadascero, Cal.: Ridgeview, 1982

Russell, B., *The Problems of Philosophy*, London: Oxford, 1986. First published 1912

Ryle, G., *Dilemmas*, Cambridge: Cambridge University Press, 1954

Salmon, W. C., *Space, Time and Motion*, 2nd edn, Minneapolis: University of Minnesota Press, 1981

   (ed.), *Zeno's Paradoxes*, New York: Irvington, 1970

Smullyan, A., *What is the Name of this Book?* Harmondsworth: Penguin, 1981

Voltaire, *Candide*, trans. J. Butt, Harmondsworth: Penguin, 1947

Winch, P., *The Idea of a Social Science*, London: Routledge & Kegan Paul, 1958

Chapter 5

Alston, W., *Philosophy of Language*, Englewood Cliffs: Prentice-Hall, 1964

Ayer, A. J., *Philosophical Essays*, London: Greenwood Press, 1980

   The Concept of a Person, London: Macmillan, 1963

Bennett, J., *Locke, Berkeley, Hume: Central Themes*, Oxford University Press, 1971

Berkeley, G., *Three Dialogues*, available in *Philosophical Works* ed. M. R. Ayers, London: Dent, 1975

196   Philosophy

Chomsky, N., 'A Review of B. F. Skinner's "Verbal Behaviour" ', in J. A. Fodor and J. J. Katz
  Cartesian Linguistics, New York: Harper & Row, 1966
  Aspects of the Theory of Syntax, Cambridge, Mass.: Massachusetts Institute of Technology Press, 1965
  Problems of Knowledge and Freedom, New York: Random House, 1972
  Language and Mind, New York: Harcourt, Brace & World, 1968
  Rules and Representations, New York: Columbia University Press, 1980
  Reflections on Language, London: Fontana, 1976
Cooper, D., *Philosophy and the Nature of Language*, London: Macmillan, 1973
  Knowledge of Language, London: Prism, 1975
Davidson, D., and G. Harman (eds.), *The Semantics of Natural Language*, Dordrecht, Reidel, 1972
Derrida, J., *On Grammatology*, trans. G. Spivak, Baltimore, Maryland: Johns Hopkins University Press, 1976
  Speech and Phenomena, trans. D. Allison, Evanston, Illinois: Northwestern University Press, 1973
Dummett, M., *The Interpretation of Frege's Philosophy*, Cambridge, Mass.: Harvard University Press, 1981 or London: Duckworth, 1981
  Truth and Other Enigmas, Cambridge, Mass.: Harvard University Press, 1978 or London: Duckworth, 1978
Feigl, H., and W. Sellars (eds.), *Readings in Philosophical Analysis*, New York: Appleton-Century-Crofts, 1949
Feyerabend, P. K., 'Against Method, a Defence of Anarchy', *Minnesota Studies in the Philosophy of Science*, IV, eds. M. Radner and S. Winokur, Minneapolis: University of Minnesota Press, 1970
  Against Method, London: New Left Books, 1975
Fletcher, P., and M. Garman (eds.), *Language Acquisition*, Cambridge: Cambridge University Press, 1980
Fodor, J. A., and J. J. Katz (eds.), *The Structure of Language*, Englewood Cliffs, New Jersey: Prentice-Hall, 1964
Frege, G., *Philosophical Writings*, trans. P. T. Geach and M. Black, Oxford: Blackwell, 1962
Guttenplan, S. (ed.), *Mind and Language*, Oxford: Clarendon Press, 1975
Hacking, I., *Why Does Language Matter to Philosophy?*, Cambridge: Cambridge University Press, 1975
Harrison, B., *An Introduction to the Philosophy of Language*, London: Macmillan 1979
Katz, J. J., *The Philosophy of Language*, London: Harper & Row, 1966
Kripke, S., *Naming and Necessity*, Oxford: Blackwell, 1981
Locke, J., *An Essay Concerning Human Understanding*, ed. P. Nidditch, Oxford: Clarendon Press, 1975; or ed. A. D. Woozley, Fontana, 1977. First published 1690
Lyas, C. (ed.), *Philosophy and Linguistics*, London: Macmillan, 1971

Lyons, J., *Chomsky*, London: Fontana, 1970

Malcolm, N., *Ludwig Wittgenstein: a memoir*, 2nd edn, Oxford: Oxford University Press, 1984

Piaget, J., *The Language and Thought of the Child*, 2nd edn, trans. M. Gabain, London: Routledge & Kegan Paul, 1948

Structuralism, trans. and ed. C. Maschler, London: Routledge & Kegan Paul, 1971

Pitcher, G. (ed.), *Wittgenstein*, London: Macmillan, 1966

Platts, M., *Ways of Meaning: an Introduction to a Philosophy of Language*, London: Methuen, 1978

Putnam, H., *Mind, Language and Reality, Philosophical Papers: Vol. 2*, Cambridge: Cambridge University Press, 1975

Meaning and the Moral Sciences, London: Routledge & Kegan Paul, 1978

Quine, W. V., 'Mind and Verbal Dispositions', in S. Guttenplan (ed.)

From a Logical Point of View, New York: Harper & Row, 2nd rev. edn, 1961

Word and Object, Cambridge, Mass.: Massachusetts Institute of Technology Press, 1960

Rhees, R., *Discussions of Wittgenstein*, London: Routledge & Kegan Paul, 1970

Rorty, R., *Philosophy and the Mirror of Nature*, Princeton, New Jersey: Princeton University Press, 1979

Russell, B., *The Problems of Philosophy*, London: Oxford, 1959. First published 1912

Logic and Knowledge, ed. R. Marsh, London: Allen & Unwin, 1977

'On Denoting', *Mind* 1905. Reprinted in H. Feigl and W. Sellars

Sampson, G., *Schools of Linguistics*, London: Hutchinson, 1980

Sapir, E., 'The Status of Linguistics as a Science', in *Culture, Language and Personality*, Berkeley: University of California Press, 1957

Language: an introduction to the Study of Speech, New York: Harcourt, 1949. First published 1921

Schwartz, S. P. (ed.), *Naming, Necessity and Natural Kinds*: Ithaca, New York: Cornell University Press, 1977

Searle, J., *Speech Acts*, Cambridge: Cambridge University Press, 1969

Skinner, B., *Beyond Freedom and Dignity*, Harmondsworth: Penguin, rev. edn, 1973

Sturrock, J., *Structuralism and Since*, London: Routledge & Kegan Paul, 1958

Wiggins, D., *Sameness and Substance*, Cambridge, Mass.: Harvard University Press, 1980

Winch, P., *The Idea of a Social Science*, London: Routledge & Kegan Paul, 1958

Wittgenstein, L., *Tractatus Logico-Philosophicus*, trans. D. F. Pears and B. F. McGuinness, London: Routledge & Kegan Paul, 1974

Philosophical Investigations, 3rd edn, trans. G. E. M. Anscombe, Oxford: Blackwell, 1968

Chapter 6

Anderson, A. Ross (ed.), *Minds and Machines*, Englewood Cliffs, New Jersey: Prentice-Hall 1964

Ayer, A. J., *Metaphysics and Common Sense*, London: Macmillan, 1967

Berlin, I., 'From Hope and Fear Set Free', *Proc. Aristotelian Society*, Vol. LXIV, 1964–5, pp. 1–29. Reprinted in *Concepts and Categories, Selected Writings, Vol. 2*, London: Hogarth Press, 1978

Boden, M. A., *Artificial Intelligence and Natural Man*, New York: Basic Books, 1977; rev. edn Cambridge, Mass.: M.I.T. Press, 1987

Borger, R., and F. Cioffi (eds.), *Explanation in the Behavioural Sciences*, Cambridge: Cambridge University Press, 1970

Brodbeck, M. (ed.), *Readings in the Philosophy of the Social Sciences*, New York: Macmillan, 1968

Carroll,Lewis, *The Annotated Alice: Alice's Adventures in Wonderland and Through the Looking Glass*, with an Introduction and Notes by Martin Gardner, New York: Bramhall House, 1960

Chappell, V. C. (ed.), *The Philosophy of Mind*, Englewood Cliffs, New Jersey: Prentice-Hall, 1962. Also available in Dover, 1982

Churchland, P. M., *Matter and Consciousness*, Cambridge, Mass.: Massachusetts Institute of Technology Press, 1984

Davidson, D., 'Thought and Talk', in S. Guttenplan (ed.)
  'The Inscrutability of Reference', in *Enquiries into Truth and Interpretation*, London: Oxford University Press, 1984
  'Truth and Meaning', in *Enquiries into Truth and Interpretation*
  'The Method of Truth in Metaphysics', in *Enquiries into Truth and Interpretation*
  Essays on Actions and Events, London: Oxford University Press, 1980

Dennett, D., *Brainstorms*, Sussex: Harvester Press, 1978

Derrida, J., *On Grammatology*, trans. G. Spivak, Baltimore, Maryland: Johns Hopkins University Press, 1976

Foucault, M., *The Order of Things*, London: Tavistock, 1974

Guttenplan, S. (ed.), *Mind and Language*, Oxford: Clarendon Press, 1975

Hofstadter, D. R. and D. C. Dennett, *The Mind's I: Fantasies and Reflections on Self and Soul*, Harmondsworth: Penguin, 1986 (first published in USA by Basic Books, Inc. 1981)

Hume, D., *A Treatise of Human Nature*, ed. E. C. Mossner, Harmondsworth: Penguin, 1985. First published 1739 and 1740

Kenny, A. J. P., *et al.*, *The Nature of Mind*, Edinburgh: Edinburgh University Press, 1972

Malcolm, N., *Problems of Mind*, London: Allen & Unwin, 1971

de la Mettrie, J., *Man a Machine*, trans. G. Bussey, Chicago: Open Court, 1977

Myers, G. E., *Self: An Introduction to Philosophical Psychology*, New York: Pegasus, 1969

Nagel, T., *Mortal Questions*, Cambridge: Cambridge University Press, 1979

O'Connor, D. J., *Free Will*, New York: Anchor Books, 1971 or London: Macmillan, 1972

Parfit, D., *Reasons and Persons*, Oxford: Oxford University Press, 1984

Place, U. T., 'Is Consciousness a Brain Process?', in V. C. Chappell (ed.)

Putnam, H., *Mind, Language and Reality: Philosophical Papers: Vol. 2*, Cambridge: Cambridge University Press, 1975

Quine, W. V., *Philosophy of Logic*, Englewood Cliffs, New Jersey: Prentice-Hall, 1970

'Mind and Verbal Dispositions', in S. Guttenplan (ed.)

Russell, B., *The Problems of Philosophy*, London: Oxford University Press, 1986. First published 1912

The Analysis of Mind, London: Allen & Unwin, 1921

Ryle, G., *The Concept of Mind*, Harmondsworth: Penguin, 1963. First published 1949

Skinner, B. F., *About Behaviourism*, London: Cape, 1975

Beyond Freedom and Dignity, rev. edn, Harmondsworth: Penguin, 1973

Walden Two, New York: Macmillan, 1976. First published 1948

Sloman, A., *The Computer Revolution in Philosophy*, Sussex: Harvester Press, 1978

Smart, J. J. C., 'Sensations and Brain Processes', in V. C. Chappell (ed.)

Strawson, P. F., 'Persons', in V. C. Chappell (ed.)

Individuals, an essay in descriptive metaphysics, London: Methuen, 1964

Tarski, A., 'The Semantic Conception of Truth', *Philosophy and Phenomenological Research* 5 (1943–4), reprinted in Feigl and Sellars (eds.) (see Biblio., Ch. 5)

Taylor, C., *Explanation of Behaviour*, Atlantic Highlands, New Jersey: Humanities Press, 1964

Turing, A., 'Computing Machinery and Intelligence', in A. Ross Anderson (ed.)

Watson, G. (ed), *Free Will*, Oxford: Oxford University Press, 1983

Williams, B., *Problems of the Self*, Cambridge: Cambridge University Press, 1973

Wittgenstein, L., *Philosophical Investigations*, 3rd edn, trans. G. E. M. Anscombe, Oxford: Blackwell, 1968

Chapter 7

Campbell, K. *A Stoic Philosophy of Life*, Lanham: University Press of America, 1986

Cicero, *On the Nature of the Gods*, trans. McGregor, Harmondsworth: Penguin, 1972

Epictetus, *Arrian's Discourses of Epictetus*, London: Heinemann, 1978

Hampshire, S., *Spinoza*, Harmondsworth: Penguin, 1951

Hicks, R. D., *Stoic and Epicurean*, New York: Russell, 1962 (reprint of 1910 edn)

Lucretius, *The Nature of the Universe*, trans. R. Latham, Harmondsworth: Penguin, 1951

Plato, *Republic*, 2nd edn, trans. D. Lee, Harmondsworth: Penguin, 1974
   Phaedrus and Letters VII and VIII, trans. W. Hamilton, Harmondsworth: Penguin, 1973

Saunders, J. L. (ed.), *Greek and Roman Philosophy after Aristotle*, New York: The Free Press, Collier Macmillan, 1966

Scruton, R., *A Short History of Modern Philosophy*, London: Routledge & Kegan Paul, 1984

Spinoza, B., *The Ethics and Selected Letters*, trans. S. Shirley, ed. S. Feldman, Indianapolis: Hackett Pub. Co., 1982. First published 1677
   Descartes' Principles, in *The Collected Works of Spinoza*, Vol. 1, ed. and trans. E. Curley, Princeton, New Jersey: Princeton U.P., 1985. First published 1663

Sprigge, T. L. S., *The Vindication of Absolute Idealism*, Edinburgh: Edinburgh University Press, 1983
   Theories of Existence, Harmondsworth: Penguin, 1984

White, R. J., *The Anti-Philosophers*, London: Macmillan, 1970

Wittgenstein, L., *Tractatus Logico-philosophicus*, trans. D. F. Pears and B. F. McGuinness, London: Routledge & Kegan Paul, 1961. First published 1921

Chapter 8

Bontempo, C. J., and S. J. Odell (eds.), *The Owl of Minerva: Philosophers on Philosophy*, New York: McGraw-Hill, 1975.

Davidson, D., 'On the very idea of a conceptual scheme', in *Enquiries into Truth and Interpretation*, Oxford: Oxford University Press, 1984

Hume, D., *A Treatise of Human Nature* ed. E. C. Mossner, Harmondsworth: Penguin, 1985. First published 1739 and 1740

James, W., *Pragmatism*, Cambridge, Mass.: Harvard University Press, 1975. First published 1907

Macintyre, A., *A Short History of Ethics*, London: Routledge & Kegan Paul, 1967

Morick, H. (ed), *Challenges to Empiricism*, London: Methuen, 1980

Passmore, J., *Recent Philosophers*, London: Duckworth, 1985

Putnam, H., *Meaning and the Moral Sciences*, London: Routledge & Kegan Paul, 1978
   Philosophical Papers, Vols. 2 and 3, Cambridge: Cambridge University Press, 1983
   Reason, Truth and History, Cambridge: Cambridge University Press, 1981
   'After Empiricism', in J. Rajchman and C. West (eds.)

Rajchman, J., and C. West (eds.), *Post-analytic Philosophy*, New York: Columbia University Press, 1985

Rorty, R., *Consequences of Pragmatism*, Sussex: Harvester Press, 1982
  Philosophy and the Mirror of Nature, New Jersey: Princeton University Press, 1980
  'Solidarity or Objectivity?', in J. Rajchman and C. West (eds.)

Russell, B., 'My mental development', in Schilpp, P. A. (ed.)

Schilpp, P. A. (ed.), *The Philosophy of Bertrand Russell*, New York: Harper & Row, 1963

Sellars, W., *Science and Metaphysics: Variations on Kantian Themes*, New Jersey: Humanities Press, 1982 or London: Routledge, 1968

Index of Philosophers and Authors Mentioned in the Text

FOR THE BEST IN PAPERBACKS, LOOK FOR THE 🐧

In every corner of the world, on every subject under the sun, Penguin represents quality and variety – the very best in publishing today.

For complete information about books available from Penguin – including Puffins, Penguin Classics and Arkana – and how to order them, write to us at the appropriate address below. Please note that for copyright reasons the selection of books varies from country to country.

In the United Kingdom: Please write to *Dept E.P., Penguin Books Ltd, Harmondsworth, Middlesex, UB7 0DA.*

If you have any difficulty in obtaining a title, please send your order with the correct money, plus ten per cent for postage and packaging, to *PO Box No 11, West Drayton, Middlesex*

In the United States: Please write to *Dept BA, Penguin, 299 Murray Hill Parkway, East Rutherford, New Jersey 07073*

In Canada: Please write to *Penguin Books Canada Ltd, 2801 John Street, Markham, Ontario L3R 1B4*

In Australia: Please write to the *Marketing Department, Penguin Books Australia Ltd, P.O. Box 257, Ringwood, Victoria 3134*

In New Zealand: Please write to the *Marketing Department, Penguin Books (NZ) Ltd, Private Bag, Takapuna, Auckland 9*

In India: Please write to *Penguin Overseas Ltd, 706 Eros Apartments, 56 Nehru Place, New Delhi, 110019*

In the Netherlands: Please write to *Penguin Books Nederland B.V., Postbus 195, NL–1380AD Weesp*

In West Germany: Please write to *Penguin Books Ltd, Friedrichstrasse 10–12, D–6000 Frankfurt/Main 1*

In Spain: Please write to *Longman Penguin España, Calle San Nicolas 15, E–28013 Madrid*

In Italy: Please write to *Penguin Italia s.r.l., Via Como 4, I-20096 Pioltello (Milano)*

In France: Please write to *Penguin Books Ltd, 39 Rue de Montmorency, F-75003 Paris*

In Japan: Please write to *Longman Penguin Japan Co Ltd, Yamaguchi Building, 2–12–9 Kanda Jimbocho, Chiyoda-Ku, Tokyo 101*